Learning

Dreamweaver CS6

with 100 practical exercises

Learning
Dreamweaver CS6
with 100 practical exercises

MCB
Press

www.mcb-press.com

Learning Dreamweaver CS6 with 100 practical exercises

Copyright © 2013 MEDIAactive

First edition: 2013

Published by © MCB Press, owned by Marcombo. Distributed in USA and Canada by ATLAS BOOKS

30 Amberwood Parkway, Ashland, Ohio 44805. To contact a representative, please e-mail us at

order@bookmasters.com.

www.mcb-press.com

Cover Designer: Ndenu

ISBN: 978-84-267-1905-8

DL: B-20392-2013

Printed in EU

Printed by Publidisa

Presentation

LEARNING DREAMWEAVER CS6 WITH 100 PRACTICAL EXERCISES

100 practical exercises that make a tour of the main functions of the program. While it is impossible to collect all the features of Dreamweaver CS6 in the pages of this book, we have chosen the most interesting and useful ones. Once you have done the 100 exercises that make up this book, the reader will be able to handle the program and create and edit complete websites, both professionally and personally, with ease.

THE WAY TO LEARN

Our experience in the field of education has lead us to design this manual, where every function is learned by carrying out a practical exercise. The exercises are explained step by step and click by click, to leave no doubts in the execution of the process. In addition, the exercises are illustrated with descriptive images of the most important steps or the results that should be obtained, and also with IMPORTANT boxes that provide further information on each of the topics covered in the exercises.

This system ensures that upon completion of the 100 exercises that make up this manual, the user will be able to cope comfortably with the basic tools of Dreamweaver CS6 and get the best out of them.

FILES REQUIRED

If you want to use the sample files that appear in this book, they can be downloaded from www.mcb-press.com.

WHO SHOULD READ THIS MANUAL

If you are starting to practice and work with Dreamweaver, you will find a complete tour of the main functions in these pages. However, if you are an expert on the program, this manual will also be very useful to see more advanced aspects or review specific functions, which you can find in the contents section.

Each exercise is treated independently, so it is not necessary to do them in order (although we recommend it, since we have attempted to group exercises thematically). Thus, if you need to address a specific issue, you will be able to go directly to the exercise where the issue is delt with and carry it out on your own computer.

DREAMWEAVER CS6

Dreamweaver is a widely recognized, standard based, computer program used to design, create and maintain applications and websites. Creating a professional looking webpage is a simple and quick task when you use the multiple and advanced tools available in Dreamweaver CS6, which is why it is one of the preferred web building programs among designers, graphic designers and web developers.

This very complete HTML visual editor will help you create complex and sophisticated dynamic web pages easily. The robust integration properties and the CSS based design, cascade style sheet, make Dreamweaver an excellent application to create and manipulate any website with ease and precision. The high quality of Dreamweaver designs is guaranteed thanks to its powerful and improved controls and tools, which you will discover through the 100 exercises that make up this handbook.

How *Learning...* books work

The title of each exercise concisely expresses what it is about. Thus, if you are interested, you can go directly to the action you want to learn or review.

The exercises have been systematically written step-by-step, so that you will never get lost during their execution.

The number to the right of the page tells you clearly in what exercise you are.

Important boxes include actions to be completed in that order to ensure that you perform the exercise correctly. They also contain information that is interesting to learn as it will facilitate your work with the program.

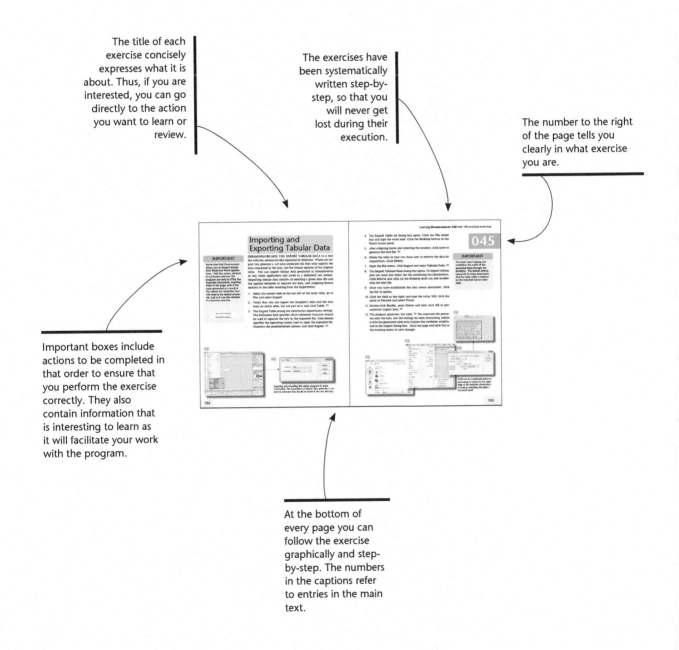

At the bottom of every page you can follow the exercise graphically and step-by-step. The numbers in the captions refer to entries in the main text.

Table of contents

Table of contents

Accessing Dreamweaver CS6

THE DREAMWEAVER CS6 Welcome Screen appears when you first start the program without any document opened or when you initiate a work session. This is a good alternative to the traditional commands for creating and opening documents. The Welcome Screen is also an easy way to access a guided tour or product tutorial for in-depth knowledge of the program's functions.

1. Click **Start** on the desktop taskbar and access Dreamweaver CS6.

2. The **Default Editor** window opens before the interface uploads. Select the documents you want edited with Dreamweaver. Maintain default settings and press **OK**.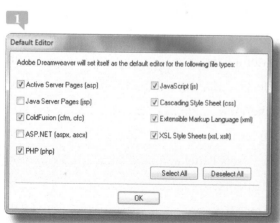

3. The application opens with the Welcome Screen in the center. 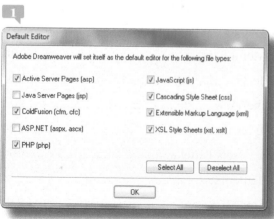 From here you can open a recent item or create a new document and search for help articles. On the bottom of the page you will find links to guide you through your first Dreamweaver steps, update you on new functions, as well as access to other resources. Go to **Open** in **Open a Recent Item**.

After you activate the Dreamweaver program for the first time you will be able to access it directly from the Start Menu.

4. The **Open** dialog box to access existing documents appears on the screen. Press **Cancel** to exit.

5. In the second group of tabs, the **Create New** tab gives you a list of common file types that create new documents quickly. Click the top option, **HTML** traditional web page format.

6. A new HTML document is automatically created. To exit, click the x button after the file name on the tab, which is, by default, **Untitled-1**.

7. The Welcome Screen reappears when you close the document. Dreamweaver CS6 has added two new features to the **Create New Tab: Fluid Grid Layout**, a system to create adaptable web design sites, and the Business Catalyst that allows you to use the integrated Dreamweaver Business panel. And last, the **Top Features (videos)** section of the Welcome Screen offers different links to tutorials of Dreamweaver CS6's main new features. Try for example the link **CS6 New Feature Overview** and view its content in your browser.

001

IMPORTANT

You can also learn about the new features and most common functions by clicking the links provided at the bottom of the pages **Getting Started** and **New Features**.

Getting Started »

New Features »

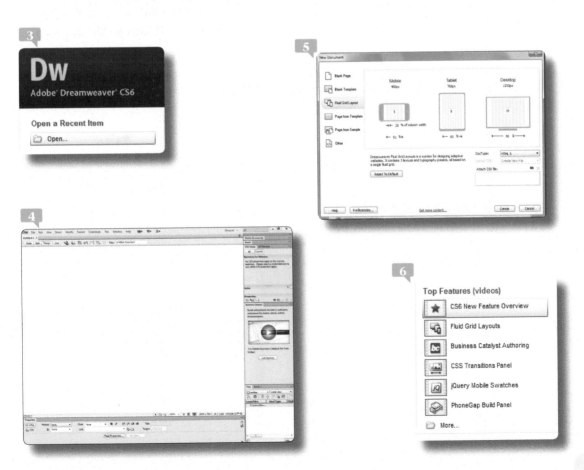

The new Dreamweaver CS6 interface

THE DREAMWEAVER CS6 INTERFACE DESIGN is intuitive and easy to use, allowing you to work quickly and rationally. The Dreamweaver workspace lets you view documents and object properties and shows all windows and panels in the same window.

1. In the document window you will find a toolbar for most common operations such as, Application Bar, Workspace switcher, and Search box. For firsthand knowledge of Dreamweaver's features click **HTML** on the Welcome Screen and create a new document. 🗩

2. Under the document tab there is the **Document toolbar** containing buttons of different document window views and visualization options such as previewing or entering a document title and other common operations. Click **Code** to change window view, 🗩 and click **Design** to return to Design view.

3. The window showing the document being created and edited occupies most of the interface space. On the lower part of the window is the **Status Bar** containing a **tag selector** and but-

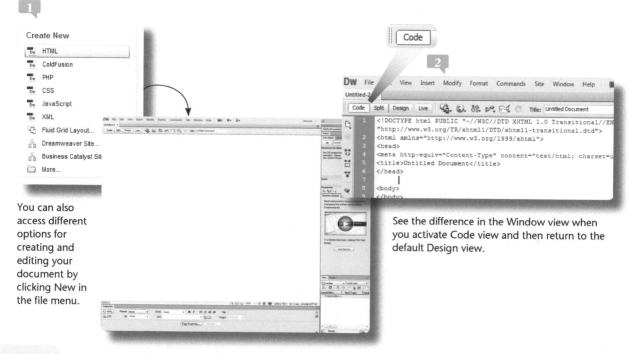

You can also access different options for creating and editing your document by clicking New in the file menu.

See the difference in the Window view when you activate Code view and then return to the default Design view.

tons to change visualization options and for document information. Under the Status Bar is the **Property Inspector,** a very useful panel that lets you view and modify the properties of the selected page, text, or object. Click **Page Properties** in the Inspector.

4. In **Page Properties** you can modify the characteristics of the page. We will go back to this point later on. For now, click **Cancel** to close.

5. To the right of the interface you will see panels to help you monitor and modify your work. Double-click the panel tab to expand or collapse panels or click the panel to switch from one to the other. Go to **AP Elements.**

6. You can also activate the panels from the Window menu. The workspace switcher in the Application Bar can be used to rearrange the workspace. Display the default **Designer** workspace and select **Coder.**

7. You will notice the same integrated workspace as in the **Designer** view but with the panels to the left, and the default **Code** view. End the exercise by returning to **Designer.**

IMPORTANT

If you have a double-monitor setup, the **Dual Screen** places all the panels on your secondary monitor while maintaining the Document window and Property Inspector open on your main monitor.

You can access the **Page Property** window from the Modify menu or click the key combination Ctrl + J.

Click the panel's tab once to expand it, or double-click to minimize it.

Creating a new document

WITH DREAMWEAVER, IN ADDITION TO HTML DOCUMENTS, you can create documents based on other server language codes (CFML, ASP, CSS) or code-based file types (Visual Basic, .NET, C#, Java). The New Document dialog box organizes files according to categories. You can create a file from scratch or use a template. You can set a default document type in the New Document category in the Preferences dialog box and automatically generate a new document based on your selection.

1. With the new blank document created in the previous exercise opened in the Dreamweaver workspace, display the **File** menu and select **New**. 🔲

2. The first column in the **New Document** dialog box is for creating a new blank page, a blank template, a template page, a fluid grid layout (new to this version of the program), a test page, or other type of document. On the right-hand side of the panel you will see a display of page types, depending on the type of document selected. The second part of the panel includes types of dynamic pages. Select the **Blank Template** category. 🔳

New...

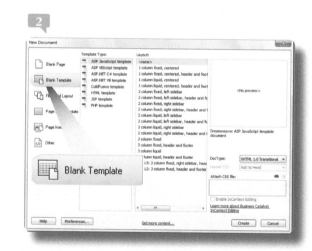

3. Here you can create your own template. Once the document is saved as a template it can be used to create others. Click **Fluid Grid Layout.**

4. In the next exercise, we will explain this new feature in CS6. Meanwhile, go to the **Page from Sample** category.

5. With CSS styles, you can assign common characteristics to all backgrounds and dialog boxes. In the **Sample Page** panel click **Colors: Red** and press **Create.**

6. The new CSS document opens in Code view. Next, click the key combination **Ctrl + N.**

7. Click on **Blank Page;** maintain the **HTML** Page Type and click on the **2 column liquid, right sidebar** option in the Layout menu.

8. It is best to set a default file type when using a certain file type for most of the pages in the same website. Go to **Preferences** and in the Default document field select the file type you want. In this case, maintain the HTML selection and click **OK.**

9. The **Get More Content** link opens the Dreamweaver Exchange where you can get more page design content. Click **Create** to create a new document.

IMPORTANT

The file types listed in the category **Other** in the **New Document** dialog box are for texts based in language codes with which it is not possible to work with visually.

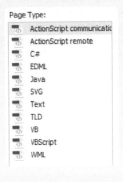

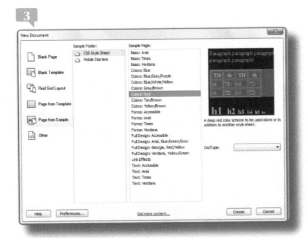

You can select your default document choice in the Dreamweaver Preferences dialog box.

Creating New Fluid Grid Layouts

ONE OF THE EXCITING NEW FEATURES IN THE CS6 VERSION is the New Fluid Grid Layout option. Accessible directly from the File menu or the New Document dialog box, the program, with an efficient CSS3-based system, provides a template for creating web designs that are compatible with various platforms and navigators.

1. Start by going to the **File** menu and then click the **New Fluid Grid Layout** button. 🔳

2. The **New Document** dialog box, with which you worked in the previous exercise, pops up and displays the **Fluid Grid Layout** file type characteristics. The main feature of this new function is the possibility of creating responsive web or page designs that automatically adjust to the viewer's device screen size, whether it is a smartphone, tablet, or desktop. The adjustment is completely graphic and percentage based from the

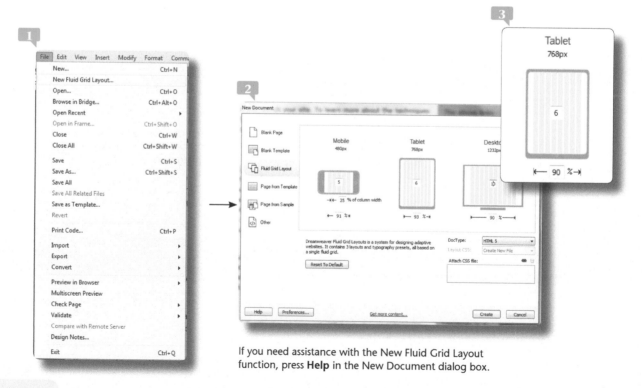

If you need assistance with the New Fluid Grid Layout function, press **Help** in the New Document dialog box.

004

window it is created in. To see how it works, change the default column number to 6. [2]

3. The percentage value immediately below the graphic indicates the portion of screen space the page or website will occupy. For the purpose of this example, reduce the value to 90%. [3]

4. If you wish to return to the original default settings after default modification, click **Reset To Default** in the dialog box. The **DocType** field, by default HTML 5, lets you select document type preferences. Display the menu to view the available options and maintain the default value. [4]

5. The **Attach CSS File** field, as its name indicates, lets you assign a CSS Styles sheet to the new document. [5] However, not having explored these elements yet, click **Create**.

6. The **Save Style Sheet File As** dialog box asking for the name and location of the new document pops up at this point. But since you won't be working with it, click **Save** without making any modifications. [6]

IMPORTANT

Once the New Fluid Grid Layout document is created, check the Status Bar for icons to change to and from available screen view modes.

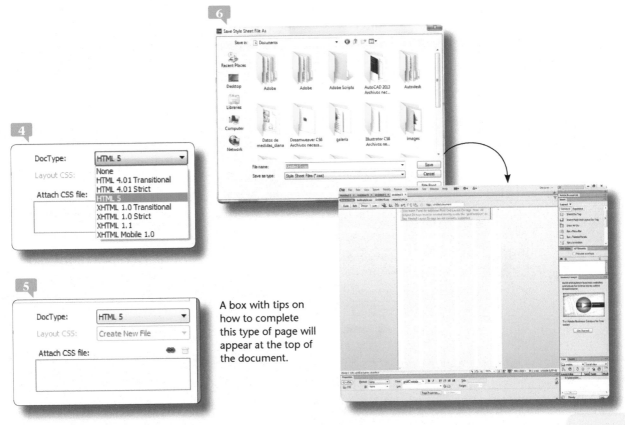

A box with tips on how to complete this type of page will appear at the top of the document.

Working with Code and Design view

DREAMWEAVER IS A VISUAL WEB PAGE EDITOR program to be used without any knowledge of the existing source code. However, you can also edit the code and enter the instructions directly. The HTML code is tag structure based. There are two page code sections: head and body. The first section contains the tags for correct Internet visualization, and the second section contains all the elements that make up the page.

1. To complete this exercise you will need to download the **sample.htm** file from our website and open it in Dreamweaver by clicking **Open** in the **File** menu.

2. The workspace configuration defines the default file view. In the **Design** workspace the default screen mode is **Design** view for documents supporting this type of visualization. Click **Code** in the **Document** toolbar.

3. The document is now set in **Code** view and can be edited directly. 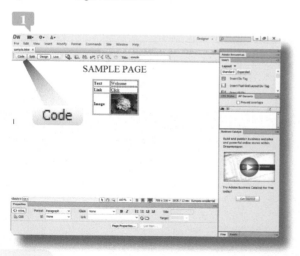 Some type of files, such as CSS styles, cannot be edited visually and must be modified by entering the code. However, HTML documents can be edited visually. Return to **Design** view.

Click the **View** menu for available options to change view modes.

4. In **Design** view you can select the page elements and work with the program's tools to define the page's appearance. Click the page image and change to **Code** view.

5. HTML language is tag based. The tag of a page element selected in **Design** view is automatically selected in **Code** view. Click **Split** in the Document toolbar to confirm. ▣

6. The **Split** mode divides the document window in two, with the code on the left-hand side, and the file's visual image on the right-hand side. Double-click one of the words on the page in the design window.

7. The **Tag Selector**, showing a series of tags in reference to the current selection, is located in the **Status Bar** at the bottom of the Document window. Click one of the tags and check to confirm if the element it defines is selected in **Design** view and if the corresponding program fragment is selected in **Code** view. ▣

8. Click **Code** in the Document toolbar and click the **Body** tag in the **Status Bar.**

9. The selection of this tag implies the selection of all the page elements. To end the exercise, click **Design view** in the Document toolbar.

005

IMPORTANT

Once published, web pages are reproduced through an Internet browser. The browser's window dimensions are according to the selected screen's resolution (pixels per inch). Dreamweaver lists window sizes indicating the browser's internal dimensions without borders. The monitor's size is in parentheses. The default sizes are applicable only when using the traditional window view. The window sizes are not applicable if the documents are in tab format.

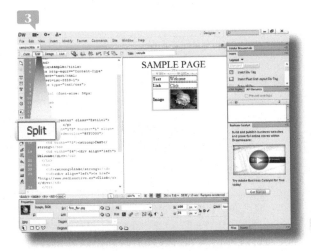

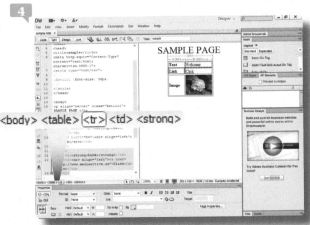

Knowing the elements of a web page

Text	Welcome
Link	Click
Image	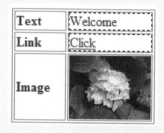

THE DREAMWEAVER DEFAULT DESIGN VIEW SHOWS ONLY the body content of the page, but you can also visually edit the head section. All tags in the header can be modified by using the Property Inspector. Head properties such as title, meta tags, or color styles, can be easily defined. Body elements can also be changed through the Properties Inspector.

1. Open the **sample.htm** document in Dreamweaver, display the **View** menu, and select **Head Content**.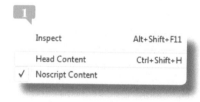

2. The visual image of the **Header** appears under the Document toolbar. To view the corresponding code, click **Split** in the Document toolbar.

3. Dreamweaver includes an icon for each head element. Select the first icon.

4. The **Title** tag is automatically selected and displayed in the properties panel. This means that the first head element is the page title and it has one single property. Be careful not to confuse page title with file name: the page title appears in the browser's **Title toolbar** when the page is published. Go to Tit-

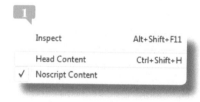

Inspect	Alt+Shift+F11
Head Content	Ctrl+Shift+H
✓ Noscript Content	

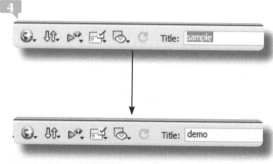

When you divide the workspace into two views, the Head elements remain in the upper part of the Design view.

You can change the page title directly in the code tag or Title field in the Properties Inspector.

006

le in the **Document toolbar** and type the word **demo.** Click **Return** to confirm the change. [1]

5. The code information is stored in a meta tag in the Head section of the document. To confirm, click the second icon in the **Head** section. [5]

6. The second tag tells the browser how to decode the document and which fonts to use. Now, go to the third element in the **Head** section. [6]

7. This section ends with a CSS style that defines format attributes of the elements contained in the body section. Click **Design** in the **Document toolbar.**

8. Your demo page includes some traditional web page elements. Double-click the word **Page** in the document's window.

9. The Properties panel shows the attributes of the current text selection. Links are also one of the principal elements in a page. Double-click the word **Click.** [7]

10. The text defined as a link appears in the **Link** field. You can also add links to images. Images are a fundamental part of web pages, enhancing and making them more attractive. Other page components are charts, sounds, videos, or other multimedia elements. Select the image to view its properties and end the exercise.

IMPORTANT

The default enabled visual aids are very helpful when completing certain actions. However, if you prefer to disable them, click in the Visual Aids menu and enable **Hide All Visual Aids**.

This information is automatically established during the creation of the document, according to the selected format.

Basic editing and saving of documents

YOU CAN SAVE DOCUMENTS under the program's default name and location, or modify both name and location in the Save As dialog box. The File menu contains commands relative to saving and storing documents; and the Edit menu contains commands relative to functions such as copy, paste, etc.

1. You modified the **sample** HTML document in the previous exercise, which is why the tab now shows an asterisk. The easiest way to save changes is to click **Save** in **File** menu. Click **Save** now.

2. The program saves changes while maintaining the original document name and location. The **Save** command is complemented by the commands **Save As, Save All, Save All Related Files,** and **Save as Template.** Open the **File** menu and click **Save As.**

3. This function saves edited documents as copies of the original. The **Save As** dialog box opens when you click **Save As** or when saving a document for the first time. You can use the dialog box to modify the name and root folder. In the **File**

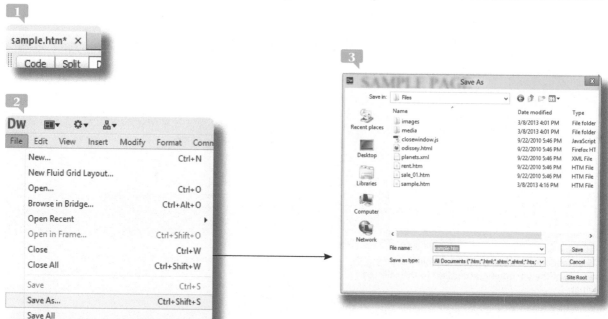

007

Name text box type the number 2 immediately following the word **sample** (no spaces) and click **Save**.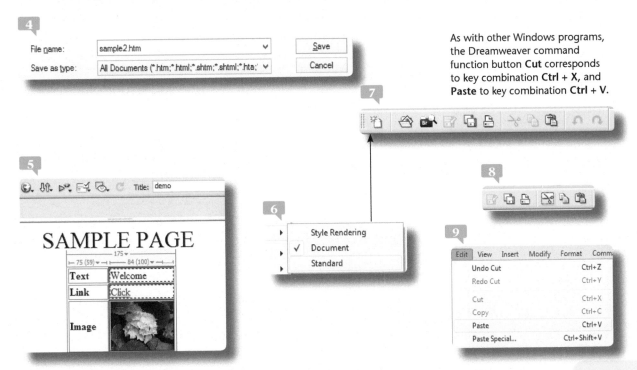

4. Click **Yes** in the new dialog box displayed to update links, regardless of whether they have been modified.

5. There are now two identical documents. The **sample2** copy is the version for editing. In the second part of the exercise we will use the Standard toolbar, by default hidden, providing direct access to commonly used **File** and **Edit** menu functions. To display it, open the **View** menu, press **Toolbar**, and click **Standard**.

6. The **Standard** toolbar is located just below the **Document** toolbar. Select the image located in the center of the page.

7. The six first **Standard** toolbar command function buttons provide direct access to **New**, **Open, Browse in Bridge, Save, Save all**, and **Print Code**, all of which are included in the **File** menu. The next group of icons corresponds to functions in the **Edit** menu. Click the icon with the scissor image to select **Cut**.

8. Now open the **Edit** menu and select **Paste**.

9. A dialog box appears where, if you wish, you can enter a text describing the image. Press **Cancel** to exit.

IMPORTANT

The **Save All** function organizes the simultaneous storage of documents in use. However, notice that the **Save as Template** function is activated only in case of a preexisting root folder site.

4

| File name: | sample2.htm | ⌄ | Save |
| Save as type: | All Documents (*.htm;*.html;*.shtm;*.shtml;*.hta; | ⌄ | Cancel |

As with other Windows programs, the Dreamweaver command function button **Cut** corresponds to key combination **Ctrl + X**, and **Paste** to key combination **Ctrl + V**.

7

5

Title: demo

SAMPLE PAGE

Text	Welcome
Link	Click
Image	

6

▸		Style Rendering
▸	✓	Document
▸		Standard

8

9

Edit	View	Insert	Modify	Format	Comm
Undo Cut					Ctrl+Z
Redo Cut					Ctrl+Y
Cut					Ctrl+X
Copy					Ctrl+C
Paste					Ctrl+V
Paste Special...					Ctrl+Shift+V

Creating a local site

A WEBSITE IS A SET OF LINKED FILES with shared characteristics such as related themes, similar design, or shared objective. Dreamweaver is a tool to create and manage complete websites as well as a visual page editor. To create a local site for a web page all you need to do is define the computer's directory that will become the site's root folder. Dreamweaver files are stored and saved in the local folder.

1. To create a new site click **Manage Sites** in the **Files** panel, located on the lower right-hand corner of the workspace,  and in the **Manage Sites** dialog box click **New Site.**

2. The **Site Setup for...** dialog box is displayed. You must first choose a name and location for your site. In the **Site Name** text field enter **Elemental.**

3. A site has a maximum of three parts or folders, depending on the developmental context and type of site selected. The local folder is the work directory. In Dreamweaver this type of folder is specified as a **Local site** and is located either in your computer equipment or network server. Click **Browse for folder** in the local site folder text box.

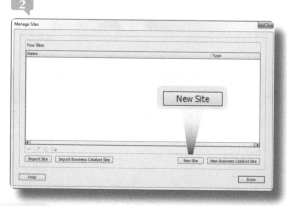

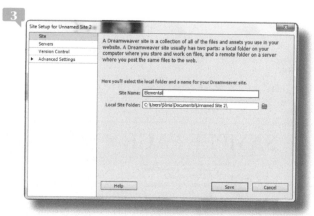

28

4. Select the location for the new site in the **Choose Root Folder** dialog box. Go to **Desktop** and click **Create new folder** and create a folder with the name **Elemental**.

5. Open the new folder and click **Select**.

6. The root folder containing the necessary files to create the website is now selected. Leave the options for advanced settings as they are and proceed to create the new site. To do this, click **Save.**

7. The new site is now in the **Manage Site** window. ⬛ From here you can edit, modify, and eliminate sites. Click **Done** to conclude the creation process of the new site.

8. To confirm the creation of the new site in the **File** panel, double-click **Elemental** in the upper part of the panel. ⬛

9. The **Site Setup for Elemental** dialog box opens ready for changes, but since there will be no modifications made, click **Cancel.** ⬛

Finally, note that in the **Manage Site** dialog box you can create new sites or eliminate those you have created. You will now access the Management Site dialog box by opening the folder panel containing the **Elemental** folder.

IMPORTANT

A web application is a set of pages that interact among themselves, with the user, and with several web servers, databases included. Click the Plus (+) button in the Servers category to activate the dialog box showing server technology. Dreamweaver supports ColdFusion, ASP. NET, ASP, JSP, and PHP for web application creation. Each of these corresponds to a specific Dreamweaver document type. The server technology you choose depends on several factors, for example your level of language programming knowledge, or the server applications setup that you use.

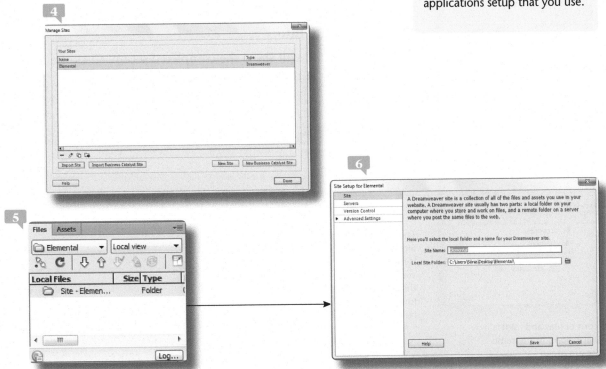

Managing local sites

IN DREAMWEAVER YOU CAN STRUCTURE A SITE before you begin to edit documents, making it easier to manage them later on. The File panel lets you view files and folders, identifying those associated with a defined site. The same site can contain different file formats. The File panel permits its generation, as well as of other file formats the program can edit.

1. Click the arrow button to the right of the word **Elemental** found in the **Show** drop-down menu of the **File** panel.

2. The **Show** drop-down menu gives you access to all sites created on the **Desktop** or on any of the computer's storage units. Click **Desktop** and press the boxed + to the left of the **Desktop items** folder.

3. Put the local website root folder, **Elemental,** in **Desktop.** Click **Manage Sites,** select the **Elemental** site and click **Edit selected site**, represented by the image of a pencil at the bottom of the dialog box.

4. Go to **Advanced Settings** in **Site Setup for Elemental** and click **Local Info.**

5. The Wizard will show the completed set up. Click the icon to the right of the **Default Images folder** field.

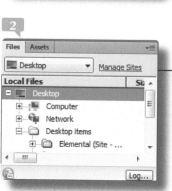

The Management Site dialog box is new to this version, although the basic program functionality remains the same.

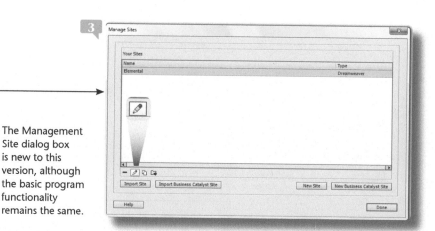

Icons of files and folders that belong to the same site are green.

6. Click **Desktop** in the access panel and double-click the Ele-mental folder icon and press **New folder**.

7. Type the word **images** and press **Return** twice.

8. Once you have created the **Elemental** site image folder, click **Select**. 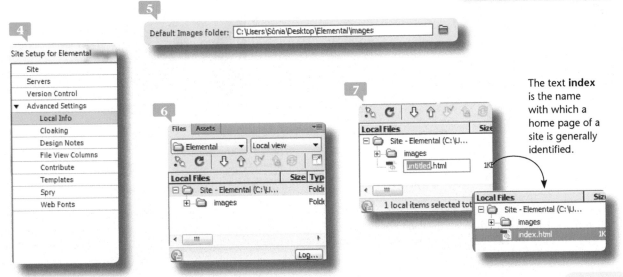 Next click **Save**, and in the **Manage Sites** dialog box click **Done**.

9. The refreshed **File** panel displays the now modified **Elemental** site. Click **Options** in the **File** panel, open the **File** submenu, and select **New File**.

10. The new document appearing in the screen will become the home page and the first page the search engine uploads. Type **index.htm** in the field box and click **Back**.

11. Right-click the **Elemental** root folder icon and then select **New Folder**.

12. Create a folder for all the home page documents; type the word **documents** and click **Return**.

13. At this point you will include only a blank page in the new folder. Right-click **Documents**, and select **New File**.

14. Type **text.htm** as the name for the new document and click **Return**.

15. To finish the exercise and close all documents, click the **Close All** command button in the **File** menu.

The text **index** is the name with which a home page of a site is generally identified.

Applying color and background image

IMPORTANT

The Properties panel allows you to create **new CSS rules** with simple explanations as to the corresponding location of the property in the style cascade without encoding.

AMONG THE VARIOUS MODIFIABLE ASPECTS of tags are background colors and title and page encoding. You can also apply a background image to a page. When you insert an image in a document the program automatically generates a reference to the file into the HTML code.

1. Double-click **index.htm** in the **File** panel.

2. Click **Page Properties** in the **Property Inspector.** 🔲

3. Since you have not yet worked with CSS styles, modify the appearance of the HTML page. Go to the panel on the left and click **Appearance (HTML).** 🔲

4. The background color of a page is an HTML property that is tag defined. Click the arrow tip in the **Background** option in the color dialog box and select a color swatch. 🔲

5. Click the **Title/Encoding** category and access content. In the field **Title** type **principal** and click **OK.** 🔲

6. Repeat the procedure with the text page, apply the same background color and name it **secondary**.

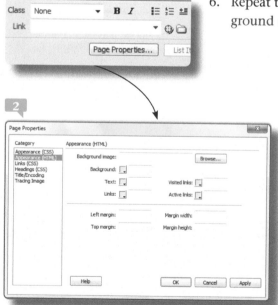

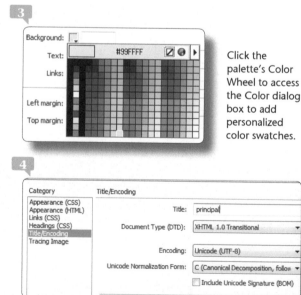

Remember that you can also access the **Page Properties** dialog box using the option in the Modify menu or by using key combination Ctrl + J.

Click the palette's Color Wheel to access the Color dialog box to add personalized color swatches.

010

7. Now apply a background image. In the **File** panel right-click the text page, select **Edit** and click **Duplicate**.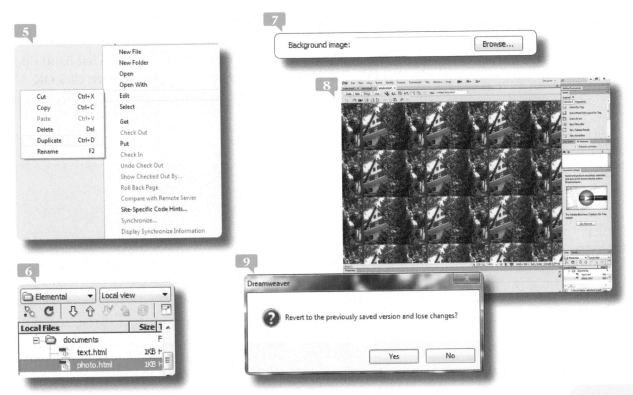

8. Rename the new copy by typing **photo.htm** and open it.

9. Click **Page Properties** in the **Property Inspector** and go to the **Appearance (HTML)** category.

10. Click the **Browse** button to the right of the **Background Image** field.

11. In **Select Image Source**, click the **Up One Level** button that displays a folder with a green arrow and create a new Desktop folder.

12. Download the necessary files from our website and save them in the new folder you can name **Dreamweaver CS6**.

13. Open this same folder from the **Select Image Source** dialog box, select the **house.jpg** file, and click **OK**.

14. In the **Page Properties** dialog box, click **OK**.

15. You have now applied the image as the screen background. To finish, open the **File** menu, click **Revert** and, in the confirmation dialog box warning that changes will be lost, click **Yes** to go back to the original document's properties.

IMPORTANT

Avoid documents with large size images, since this increases downloading time; also, reduced image backgrounds are better for content visualization.

33

Design Notes and Tracing Images

THE TRACING IMAGE CATEGORY in Page Properties allows you to select an original image document. For correct visualization of page elements, set a transparency value before using the tracing image application. Design Notes are comments you write about a file. They are associated with the file, but stored separately. Design Notes keep track of all the information associated with the files.

1. Click the **index.htm** document, 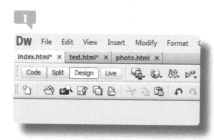 go to **Page Properties** and enable the **Tracing Image** category.

2. You need to specify the directory where the document to be used as a tracing image is located. Click **Browse**.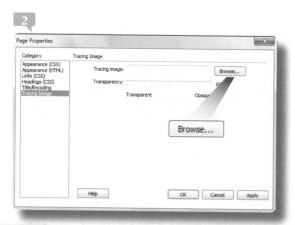

3. In the **Select Image Source** dialog box find and select the **reference.jpg** document and click **OK**.

4. The program copies the document to the site directory assigned to store this type of file. Click **OK**.

5. The image remains embedded in the background as a visual guide to facilitate editing and correct page structuring. 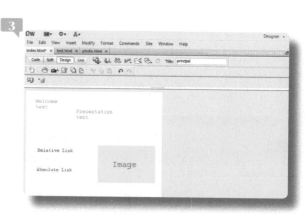 Go back to the **Page Properties** dialog box and enable **Tracing Image**.

6. Tracing Images are opaque by default. Click the left-hand side of the **Transparency** slider and set at **20%** opacity; click **OK**.

A Tracing Image is a reference only, and it is not visible when you view the page in a browser.

Although not visible when viewing in a browser, the files used as Tracing Images are automatically stored in their corresponding site folder.

7. The image now serves as a guide without any of the inconveniences. You will now learn about Design Notes, another type of work control help. Open the **File** menu and select **Design Notes**.

8. Design Notes can be used to keep track of any extra information associated with documents, like comments on the status of the file. In the **Notes** text box type the words **Erase reference**.

9. Design Notes can also be used to keep track of confidential information you cannot enter in a document for security reasons. Enable the **Show when file is opened** option.

10. The note is now activated and will appear before you start editing the associated document. Click **OK**.

11. Close the **index.html** file and, in the pop-up warning dialog box, click **Yes** to save the changes.

12. In the **Files** panel double-click **index.html** to reopen the document and verify the program does, in fact, display the corresponding Design Note before uploading the page for editing. Disable **Show when file opens** and click **OK**.

13. Go back to the **Page Properties** dialog box and enable the **Tracing Image** category, select field path and press **Delete** to eliminate it. Click **OK**.

IMPORTANT

The **All Info** tab in the Design Notes dialog box shows the name and location of the file associated with a given Design Note. Use the + button to add new elements to the note, defining values in the Name and Value dialog box. Remove elements selected in the Information dialog box with the – button.

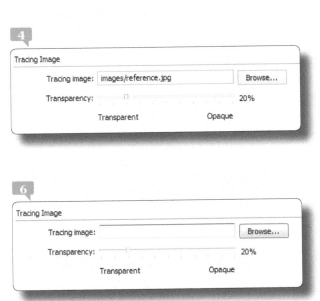

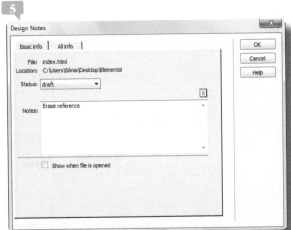

You can also access the Design Notes dialog box using the contextual menu of the document you want to associate the note to.

Exporting and deleting sites

DREAMWEAVER SAVES YOUR SITE SETTINGS in folders that are meant to store users' data information. But in today's world the need to transfer information for any number of reasons, such as team work or other job requirements, is more and more frequent. With Dreamweaver's .ste file extensions you can easily export the settings of all your sites. These files store only site settings, not the files that compose it, which means that in case of deletion only the site's settings are deleted.

1. Press the arrow button of the **Show** dialog box in the **File** panel and select **Desktop**.

2. Once the settings are defined you can create the site's basic structure: main page and two folders containing documents and images. Click the **Manage Sites** link in the **File** panel. 🗩

3. You can use site settings saved in Dreamweaver at any time and in any computer. Go to the **Elemental** site you created in earlier exercises and click **Export** (fourth icon below the Site panel). 🗩

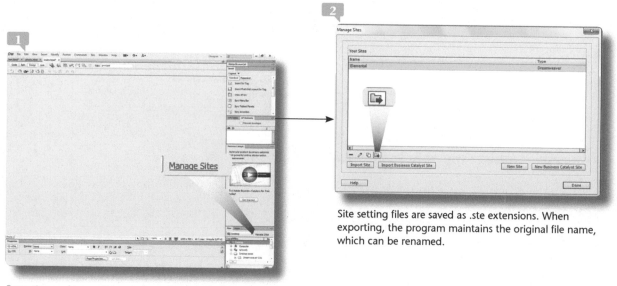

Site setting files are saved as .ste extensions. When exporting, the program maintains the original file name, which can be renamed.

Exporting and Importing are done through the **Manage Sites** dialog box.

012

4. In the **Export Site** dialog box select the directory where you want to store the site's settings. Click **Desktop** in the Access panel and click **Save**.

5. Delete the **elemental** site after exporting the settings. Press **Delete** (the first icon below the Site panel).

6. The settings cannot be restored once deleted. Click **Yes** to delete forever and press **Done** in the **Manage Sites** dialog box.

7. To finish the exercise, change the location of the folder containing the site structure. Open the **File** menu and select **Close All**; click **Yes** in the two dialog boxes appearing on the screen to save the changes made.

8. Right-click the **elemental** folder in the **Files** panel, click **Edit** and in the contextual menu select **Cut**.

9. Place the folder in a new folder you will open in the **Desktop**. Right-click the **Desktop Elements** folder and, in the contextual menu, click **New folder**.

10. Use this folder to store the various sites created with these exercises. Type the word **sites** and press **Return**.

11. Right-click the **sites** folder, click the **Edit** menu again and select **Paste**. Verify that the elemental folder content has been correctly transferred.

Press the boxed + to the left of the folder to verify that the folders have been correctly pasted.

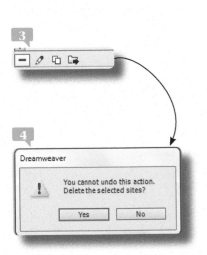

When you delete a site, only the site's settings are deleted, the folder structure and files composing the site are saved.

Be careful when using the Cut command button: a second use of it erases the first cut element's information stored in the Clipboard. Also, depending on the version of your operating system, you risk losing the original element.

Importing sites

YOU CAN IMPORT DREAMWEAVER SITE SETTINGS to the original computer or to any other computer and recuperate your site settings information at any time. To facilitate importing, the documents contained in the .ste file must be structured in the same manner as the documents in the computer doing the importing. If the site root folder is not in the same directory as it was when the site file was created, you need to identify the new root folder and image folder (if you decide to use this recourse).

1. In this exercise, you will practice importing the saved settings. In the **Manage Sites** dialog box in the **Files** panel, click **Import Site**.

2. In the **Import Site** dialog box double-click the **Elemental** site icon.

3. The information relative to the whereabouts of the previous root folder is in the .ste document, so the program does not know how to locate the root folder in the directory it was in when the site was exported. In the dialog box displayed you can select the root folder. Open the **sites** folder and repeat this with the **Elemental** folder.

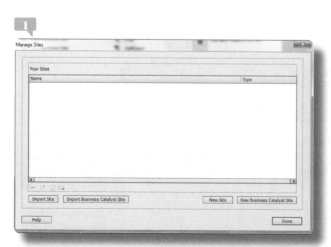

Settings defined in the various categories of the Site Definition dialog box are saved when importing a site.

Site structure information is saved to a memory denominated cache for easier management of the documents associated with a site.

4. Click **Select** to make the **elemental** folder the imported site's root folder.

5. The loss of the root folder's reference also implies the loss of the image folder's reference. In the dialog box double-click the **images** folder and click **Select**.

6. The program uploads the new site's settings. Click **Done**.

7. When the directory location of the root folder is modified, the program is required to regenerate the information relative to its structure to be able to display it correctly in the **File** panel. Click the boxed + beside the site's root folder to open it.

8. The entire content appears in the green color, which is associated with a certain site.  To access the files contained in a site, press the arrow button of the **Show** dialog box in the **File** panel, and select **Manage Sites**.

9. With the **Elemental** site selected, click **Edit**.

10. In **Advanced Settings** go to **Design Notes** and confirm the option indicating they must be saved, even though they are not activated, is selected. In the **Maintain Design Notes** option select the verify box to disable. Click **Yes** in the pop-up dialog box.

11. Click **Save** and in the **Manage Sites** dialog box click **Done**.

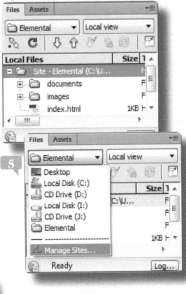

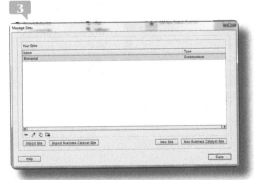

To modify the properties of a site, go to the Manage Sites dialog box and click Edit.

An active Design Note is automatically displayed when the associated document is opened. When you click Clear Design Notes you delete the _notes folder and its entire contents.

When you press the Yes button you delete all the Design Notes included in that site.

Duplicating and editing sites

DUPLICATING A SITE IS NOT TO BE CONFUSED with duplicating the documents composing the site. A site duplicate is a copy of the original settings you can later edit. You can also adjust the duplicate to create a site similar to the original. Drag the files of a site to duplicate directly in the File panel. To correctly finish the operation, the duplicate destination folder must belong to a site.

1. In this exercise you will see the difference between a site's settings duplicate and a site's content duplicate. Go to **Manage Sites,** select the **Elemental** site and click **Duplicate,** the third icon in the group below the Sites panel. 🔲

2. By default, the program names the duplicate **Elemental copy, which is now selected.** 🔲 Click **Edit.**

3. In the **Site Name** field, type **styles** and click the folder icon to the right of the **Local Site Folder** field. 🔲

4. To avoid confusion and facilitate site management, the settings should be assigned to a new folder. In the **Sites** folder, click **New folder.**

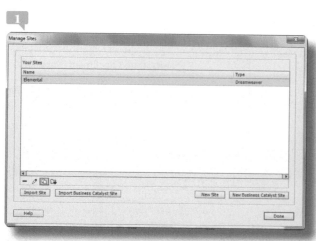

A site's settings duplicate does not imply the duplication of the files composing it.

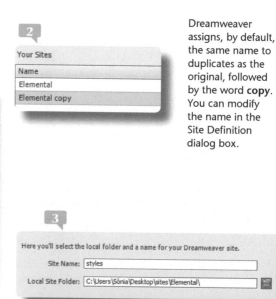

Dreamweaver assigns, by default, the same name to duplicates as the original, followed by the word **copy.** You can modify the name in the Site Definition dialog box.

3

Here you'll select the local folder and a name for your Dreamweaver site.

Site Name: styles

Local Site Folder: C:\Users\Sònia\Desktop\sites\Elemental\

5. Use the same name assigned to the duplicate. Type the word **styles,** then click **Return,** go to **Open** and press **Select.**

6. Delete the image folder reference. In **Advanced Settings** go to **Local Info,** select the defined folder and click **Delete.**

7. In the Settings dialog box click **Save,** and in the Management dialog box click **Done.**

8. Open the **Show** dialog box and select **Desktop.**

9. Duplicate and save the structure of all the **Elemental** site's files contained in the **styles** folder. In the **Files** panel open the **Elemental** folder. Press the **Shift** key to select all of the files.

10. In the **Files** panel click **Edit** and **Copy.**

11. Right-click the **styles** site, click **Edit** and **Paste.**

12. The program automatically duplicates the original files. Display the **Show** dialog box and select **styles.**

13. Click the boxed + to the left of the site to verify its structure.

14. To finish, select the **image** folder, click **Delete** and **Yes** in the **Confirmation** dialog box.

When deleting the image folder default route, an Alert Box automatically pops up because the program cannot locate the folder in the site. Press Accept to continue.

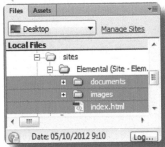

You can duplicate a site's file directly in the **Files** panel using the drag option. To correctly finish this action, the duplicate destination folder must also belong to a site.

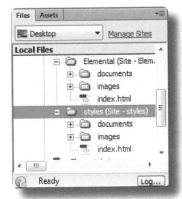

To select several elements at the same time in the File panel, press the Shift key when clicking the elements.

Inserting text

THE TEXT IS THE MAIN COMPONENT of a web page and has practically no impact in the downloading time of the page. In Dreamweaver, as a general practice, you can't insert two consecutive blank spaces. The text areas of a page are divided into paragraphs that are automatically created when you press the Enter key. Web browsers automatically insert a blank line of space between paragraphs. But with Dreamweaver you can add a single blank line of space between paragraphs by inserting a line break when you press Shift + Enter.

1. Practice with the **Elemental** site you've been working with. Start by editing the home page. Activate the **Elemental** site in the **File** panel and double-click to open **index.htm**.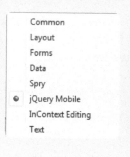

2. The edit cursor is positioned on the first line of the document when there is no content. Type the word **house** and press the keyboard's **space bar.**

3. Hit the **space bar** a second time to verify that you cannot insert two consecutive blank spaces. Type the words **house for sale** to complete the phrase and click **Enter.**

4. You have now created a second paragraph. A tag, **<p>**, identifying the paragraph element, appears in the **Status Bar.** Type the text, **visit our web.**

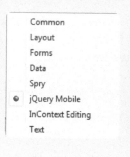

Dreamweaver jumps to the next line when the text reaches the right margin of the page.

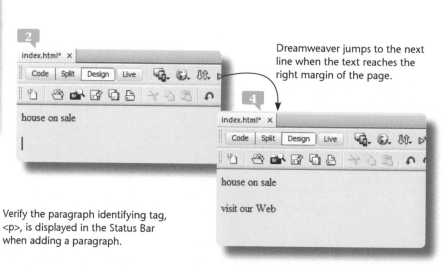

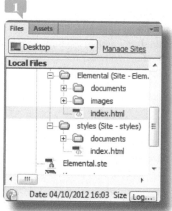

Verify the paragraph identifying tag, <p>, is displayed in the Status Bar when adding a paragraph.

5. Generally, there is a blank line between paragraphs because web browsers automatically insert it to separate the various text blocks in a page, but the program lets you insert what is referred to as a line break. Open the **Insert** menu; click the **HTML** option, select **Special Characters** and click the **Line Break** command button. **5**

6. The new line belongs to the same paragraph as the line before it and there are no blank lines between the two. Click the **Back** key.

7. Press **Shift + Enter** to introduce a line break with the keyboard and type the example text, **expand image**. **6**

8. The **Insert** panel permits the inclusion of diverse elements organized in categories. Display the default field category **Layout 7** and click **Text**. **8**

9. The options let you insert text related to HTML tags. **9** In the **Characters** option, which includes all special characters, select **Line Break**. **10**

10. Save the changes. It is a good practice to do this regularly to avoid accidental losses. Remember that if you want to save the document in its original state, you can use the **Save** command to create a copy. Click the **Save** command icon with the disk image in the Standard toolbar.

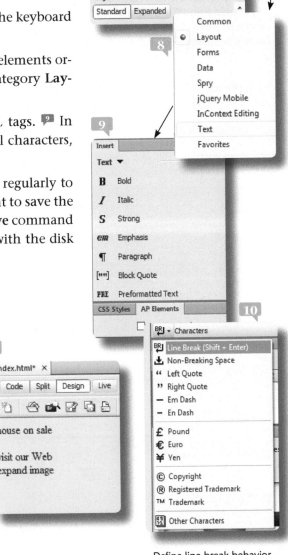

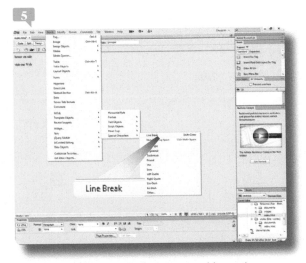

The Line Break command allows you to add a carriage return without changing paragraphs.

Define line break behavior in the Character dialog box.

Copying and pasting text

COPYING AND PASTING text save time. Among the several different kinds of text formats professionals receive to incorporate in a web page are ASCII text files, Enriched Text Format (ETF), and Office documents.

1. To complete the exercise, copy the **presentation** and **description** files found on our website. Minimize the Dreamweaver window and open the folder with the copied documents.

2. The downloaded sample files were created with the WordPad application included in the Windows operating system. Press the Shift key to select the entire **presentation** text. Right-click the selection and press **Copy**. Once the text is copied, click the close button in the application **Title Bar**.

3. Back in Dreamweaver, click the top of the first text line, open the **Edit** menu and select **Paste**.

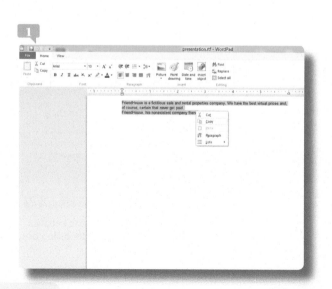

016

4. To separate the pasted text from the preceding text, press **Enter**.

5. Next, select the first words **FriendHouse** and, in the Standard toolbar, click **Copy**. 3

6. Click the top of the line and press **Paste** in the Standard toolbar. 1 For the new words to constitute an independent paragraph, press **Enter**.

7. Click **Save**, in the Standard toolbar, to store changes made to the page. 5

8. In the **Files** panel, click the boxed + to the left of the **documents** folder to expand it and double-click the **text.html** document to open it.

9. Now copy new text from the second document sample. Open the document **description.rtf**, select and copy the entire text. Return to Dreamweaver.

10. With the **text.html** page expanded, go to the **Edit** menu and select **Paste**.

11. Dreamweaver does not respect the original text format. The pasted text maintains the same font used in the **index.htm** document including that of the pasted text from the **presentation** file. 6 To finish the exercise, Click **Save** to store the changes.

IMPORTANT

To select the entire content of a page, click the body tag or execute the Select All command or shortcut key combination Ctrl + A.

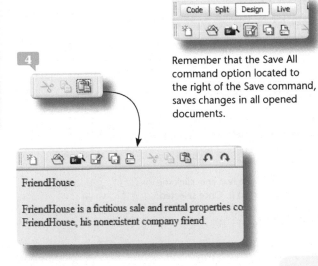

To select a paragraph fragment click the first letter and drag it to the end of the desired fragment. To select a complete paragraph, press the <p> tag in the tag selector.

Remember that the Save All command option located to the right of the Save command, saves changes in all opened documents.

Modifying text format

THE TEXT BLOCKS of a page are formatted as paragraphs. To select an entire paragraph directly click the <p> tag in the Status Bar. This format has a predetermined font style and size. Dreamweaver lets you define the format of each text block accordingly by using headings. A heading defines a series of characteristics, font size, and style of a given text block.

1. Click the left margin of the first line in the page to select it and press the **Copy** icon in the Standard toolbar. 🔲

2. Activate the **index.htm** page and with the editing cursor at the end of the page, click the **Paste** icon in the Standard toolbar.

3. Dreamweaver lets you apply different formats to the paragraphs of a page. Select the first words, **FriendHouse**; open the **Format** menu and in the **Paragraph Format** option click **Preformatted Text**. 🔲

4. Paragraph formats define text characteristics such as font style and size, although considering that the text visualized in Dreamweaver often differs from what the browser shows, these definitions are somewhat relative. Use the **Insert** panel to apply a heading format to a paragraph. Click the **h1** option in the panel. 🔲

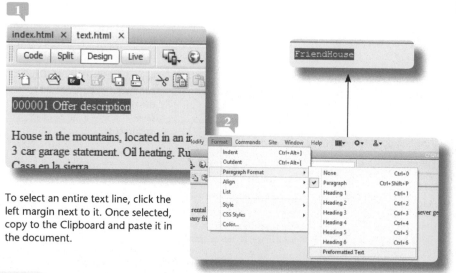

To select an entire text line, click the left margin next to it. Once selected, copy to the Clipboard and paste it in the document.

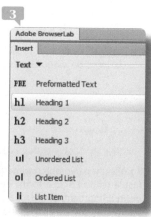

5. The selected text is now defined as Heading Style 1 and the corresponding **h1** tag appears in the Status Bar.  This type of heading also defines text size and bold text application. Click the end of the selected word to see the results.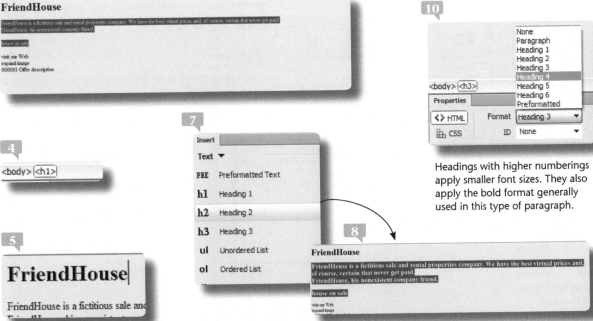

6. Press **Enter** to verify that the program creates new paragraphs without applying the previous format, as established in your preferences.

7. Modify the format of the following two paragraphs. Click **Delete** to eliminate a carriage return and select the next three text lines, up until the word **sale**.

8. To define the selected paragraphs as headings, click **h2**.

9. The font size in h2 is smaller than h1. Select the first two words in the text selected and, in the **Insert** panel, click **h3**.

10. The **h3** tag in the Status Bar lets you select the entire text associated to that heading. Click it.

11. You can also use the Properties panel to apply paragraph and heading formats to a text. In the **Format** field, in the Properties panel, click the arrow button and select **Heading 4**.

12. Place the cursor at the end of the selection and, in the Standard toolbar, click the **Save** icon.

<body> <h3>

The None option removes all format options applied to a paragraph.

Headings with higher numberings apply smaller font sizes. They also apply the bold format generally used in this type of paragraph.

Changing text color and properties

DREAMWEAVER'S TEXT DEFAULT FONT, as defined in the Preference dialog box, is Times New Roman in black. The program lets you change font style, color, and size.

1. Open the **Edit** menu, click **Preferences** and go to **Font**.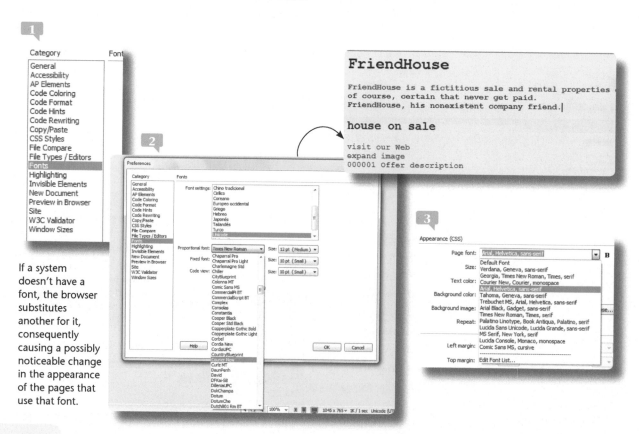

2. The upper part of the dialog box is reserved for **Font Settings** specifying the Dreamweaver font combination for documents using a specific encoding type. Open the **Proportional font** field menu, select **Courier New** and click **OK**.

3. You can also change font preferences in the **Page Properties** dialog box by clicking the **Proportional Font Property Inspector** button.

4. Click the **Page Font** field arrow and select **Arial, Helvetica, sans-serif.**

If a system doesn't have a font, the browser substitutes another for it, consequently causing a possibly noticeable change in the appearance of the pages that use that font.

5. Next, click the (HTML) **Appearance** category, open the **Text** field and select a sample from the panel.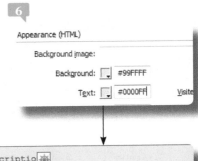

6. Press **OK** to apply the font and color.

7. Apply the first font from the selected list. Save the **index.htm** changes and maximize the **text.htm** page.

8. Go back to **Page Properties**, click the arrow in the **Size** list field and select, for example, value **14**.

9. Next, select the **Appearance (HTML)** category in the panel to the left of the dialog box.

10. Colors in HTML are expressed in **hexadecimal** values. The program uses these values to define a specific color tone. In the **Text** field insert hex color value **#0000FF** and accept the changes.

11. Next, apply a defined style to the selected text. Select the first text line on the page and click the **Bold** command symbol B in the **Properties** panel.

12. Click the **Save** icon in the Standard toolbar to save changes.

IMPORTANT

Browsers use the first font found in the font combination installed in the user's system, going down the list until one coincides.

000001 Offer descriptio

House in the mountains, located in an incomparable s
and basement of 20 m2.

000001 Offer description

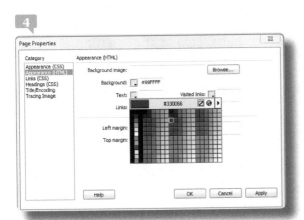

Page Properties

Category: Appearance (HTML)

Appearance (CSS)
Appearance (HTML)
Links (CSS)
Headings (CSS)
Title/Encoding
Tracing Image

Background image: Browse...
Background: #99FFFF
Text: #330066
Links: Visited links:
Left margin:
Top margin:

Help   OK   Cancel   Apply

FriendHouse

FriendHouse is a fictitious sale and rental properti
paid.

Creating InContext editing files

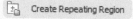

IMPORTANT

Use the **Create Repeating Region** option to define the structure and properties of an area of a page that the user can copy and add content to when editing in a browser.

Create Repeating Region

THE DREAMWEAVER INCONTEXT EDITING is an online editing service that lets users make simple content changes within a browser without the need for other software or assistance from the web's developer. This online service can be applied to a specific region or pages according to personalized formatting options.

1. The HTML **ice:editable** (InContext Editable) tag identifies the area the user can edit. To complete this exercise add an editable region below the first line of the **text.htm** page. Click the end of the first sentence and press **Enter** to create a new paragraph.

2. Access InContext Editing directly from the **Insert** panel or **Insert** menu. Display the category list in the **Insert** panel, select **InContext Editing** 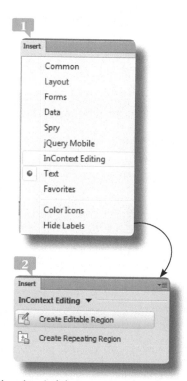 and click **Create Editable Region**.

3. Select **Insert new Editable Region at the current insertion point** in the **Create Editable Region** dialog box and click **OK**.

4. Dreamweaver automatically adds a **div** tag (container that includes text, images, charts, etc.) at the insertion point, as

Dreamweaver offers options that vary according to your preferences.

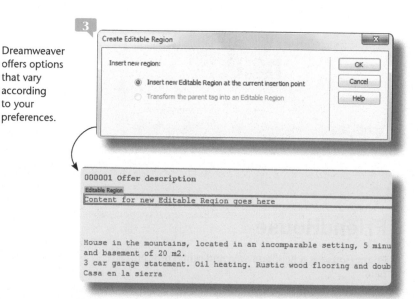

Keep in mind that you can access these functions in the InContext Editing submenu of the Insert menu.

shown in the Tag Selector Bar. In addition, the **Properties** panel lists the formatting tools available for this type of region. The user will be able to edit the selected area directly in the browser using the options enabled by the developer. For example, let's say the only thing you want users to be able to edit is the screen's background color. Click **Uncheck All** 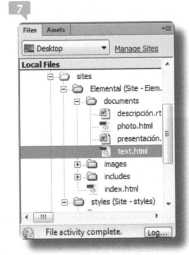 and select the **Background Color** checkbox. **5**

5. Click the **Save** button in the toolbar to save the changes.

6. The first time you save a document with an InContext Editing functionality, Dreamweaver displays the **Copy Dependent Files** dialog box informing you that the supported added files must be uploaded to the server so that they can be edited in the browser. Click **OK**. **6**

7. To see what the generated file folder **includes**, press the F5 key to refresh the panel. **7**

8. Once you've set up a remote server to publish your page on, use the **Place** option in the folder's contextual menu to add InContext Editing files so that they may be edited directly in the browser. To remove the region's encoding click **Remove Region** in the **Properties** panel.

9. The verification dialog box tells you that, although the region will be removed, its contents will be saved. Click **OK** and click **Save** to save the changes.

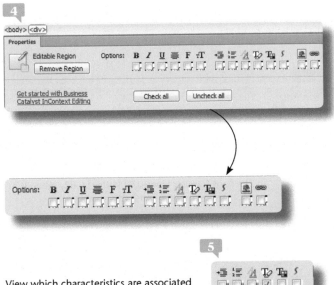

View which characteristics are associated to which options in the Properties panel.

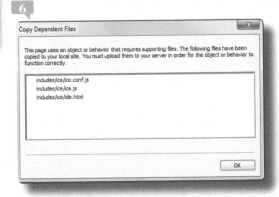

InContext Editing supports ice.conf.js, ice.js, and ide.html.

Importing and using web fonts

IMPORTANT

To modify a predetermined font folder containing a site's additional fonts, from the File panel, go to the **Web Fonts** category of the site's Settings dialog box.

Templates
Spry
Web Fonts

A NEW FEATURE IN DREAMWEAVER CS6 is the possibility of importing creative Internet supported fonts. You can use the program's web font manager to import selected fonts that you can then use on your website. Among others, Dreamweaver supports Google and Typekit fonts.

1. In this exercise you will learn how to import web fonts. Open **index.htm**.

2. Go to the **Modify** menu and select **Web Fonts**.

3. In the **Web Fonts Manager** dialog box displayed select **Add Fonts**.

4. Another dialog box, the **Add Web Font** dialog box, opens. Select the font you want to use in this box. The Internet has thousands of font sites, some of them are free (Google), and others you need to pay for (Typekit). Whatever your selection, you will need the folder containing the downloaded

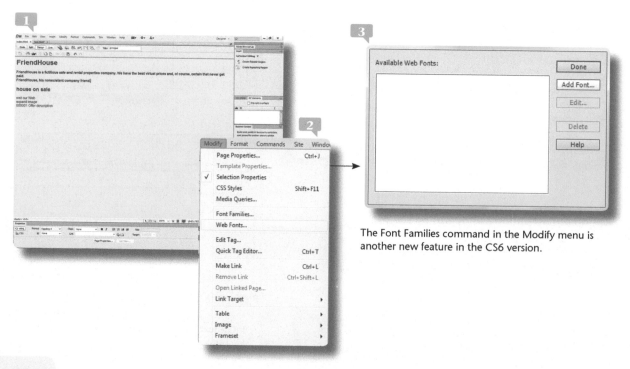

The Font Families command in the Modify menu is another new feature in the CS6 version.

020

fonts stored on your computer. For the purposes of this exercise you can use the font in the computer's folder. In the **Add Web Font** dialog box click the **EOT Font** folder icon, and press the font's corresponding command button in the **Open** dialog box.

5. The font is now added to the **Add Web Font** dialog box. Select the option located below the file fields to verify you are authorized to use the font and click **OK**.

6. The font is now displayed in the Web Fonts Manager dialog box. Click **Done** to finalize process.

7. Although apparently nothing has changed, the new font has in fact been added to the list of available fonts. To verify, click the **CSS** option in the **Properties** panel and display the **Font** field. The web font is now contained within a group of independent fonts.

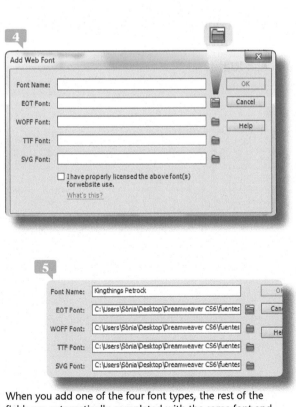

When you add one of the four font types, the rest of the fields are automatically completed with the same font and in the corresponding format.

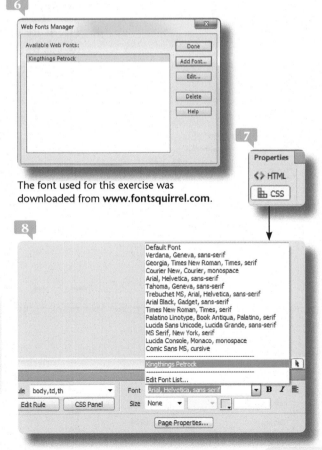

The font used for this exercise was downloaded from **www.fontsquirrel.com**.

Changing margins and text alignment

DREAMWEAVER LETS YOU SET THE TOP AND LEFT MARGINS of a page. To do this, go to the Page Properties dialog box and select the HTML Appearance category. To align an entire paragraph in relation to the margins, use the four command buttons displayed in the Format/Align menu or in the Property Inspector in CSS view.

1. Open **text.htm**, click **Page Properties** and go to the **HTML Appearance** category. ▮1

2. You will see four possibilities, although only the left and top margins can be set. Enter the value **20** in the **Left margin** field box. ▮2

3. Margin values are in pixels. Enter the value **30** in the **Top margin** field and press **OK**. ▮3

4. There are four alignment options, left, right, center, and justify. Go to the **Format** menu and select **Align**. ▮4

5. In the submenu, click **Right**.

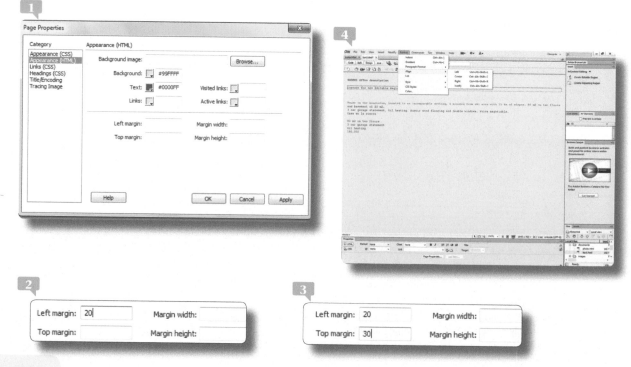

6. The entire paragraph is automatically aligned to the right.
   Next, open **index.htm**.

7. Set the same margins as in the previous document. In the Properties panel click **Page Properties**.

8. Activate the **Appearance (HTML)** category and enter the value 20 in the **Left margin** field box.

9. Enter the value 30 in the **Top margin** field box and click **OK**.

10. Click next to the start of the first paragraph, display the **Format** menu, select **Align** and select **Right**.

11. Click the beginning of the second paragraph, press the **CSS** command button in the Properties Panel 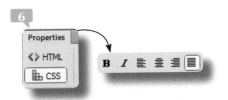 and click **Justify**, the last command button in the **Properties** panel list.

12. Changes made in the CSS Style Sheet affect the entire page. Verify by clicking the beginning of the fourth paragraph and, in the Properties panel activate **Align Center**.

13. To align the selected paragraph to the left, go to the **Format** menu, click **Align** and select **Left**.

14. Finish the exercise by clicking **Save** in the Standard toolbar.

IMPORTANT

Enter the margin settings in the corresponding Margin width and Margin height fields so that other browsers do the same. Enter the value 0 if you don't want margins showing in browsers.

Margin width:

Margin height:

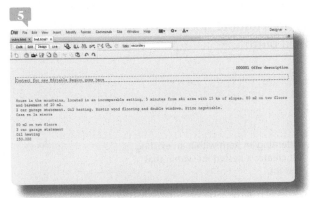

By default, paragraphs are aligned to the left.

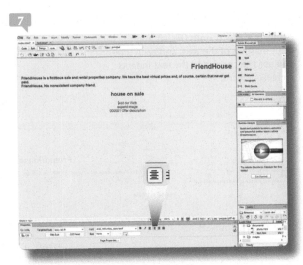

Paragraphs are justified flush with both the left and right margins.

Creating lists and indenting text

DREAMWEAVER LETS YOU INDENT THE DIFFERENT text blocks of a page. Indenting means you move both margins of the selected text inward, away from the page's main margins. To add or delete indents use the first two options in the Format menu or the corresponding commands in the Properties panel. The program also allows you to insert bulleted or numbered lists, simplifying the creation of outlines. You can also create a nested (a list within a list) definition list.

1. With the cursor at the beginning of the second paragraph go to the **Format** menu, click **Align** and select **Left**.

2. Activate the **HTML** option in the Properties panel and select **Blockquote**, shown as a series of lines preceded by an arrow pointing to the right.

3. The blockquote tag appears in the Status Bar selector. Click **Blockquote** again.

4. You can apply multiple indents to a paragraph. Each time you do the text indents farther from both sides of the document. Click **Remove Blockquote**, located to the left of the Blockquote command button.

You can apply multiple indents to the same paragraph. The Indent Text command affects both the left and right margins of the text, and each time you use the command the text indents increase inward.

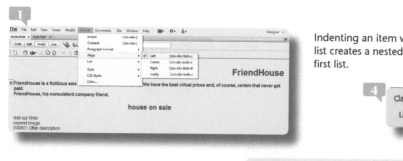

Indenting an item within an existing list creates a nested list within that first list.

5. Click the fourth paragraph, go to the **Format** menu and select **Indent**.

6. Explore another page formatting option. Go to **List** in the **Format** menu and click **Unordered List**.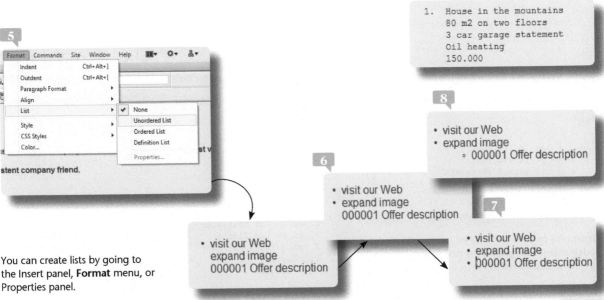

7. Unordered lists create paragraphs preceded by bullet points; in this case a small round circle. The list consists of one paragraph and, therefore, one item. Place the cursor after the term **Web**, press **Delete** and click **Enter**. This creates a new paragraph and adds a new item to the list.

8. Repeat with the word **image**, clicking **Delete** and **Enter** as explained above.

9. There are now three items in the list, all three at the same level and preceded by a bullet. Press **Blockquote** in the Properties panel.

10. When you indent an item within a list you automatically create a new list within the original list identified by a new bullet symbol. Dreamweaver also lets you create nested **definition lists**. Click **Remove Blockquote**.

11. Open the **text.htm** document.

12. Place the cursor at the beginning of the fourth paragraph, activate the **Text** option in the **Insert** panel and click **ol, Ordered List**.

13. Click **Save** to store your changes and finish the exercise.

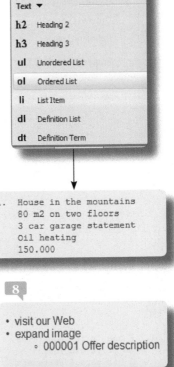

You can create lists by going to the Insert panel, **Format** menu, or Properties panel.

Creating list styles and items

IMPORTANT

The **List** submenu in the Format menu contains all the command buttons needed to create and delete lists. The **None** option deletes lists from the selected paragraphs. There is also an option for each different type of list.

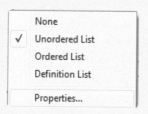

DREAMWEAVER LETS YOU CREATE ORDERED, unordered, and definition lists. Definition lists don't use bullets or numbers, and are generally used in glossaries or descriptions. Indent an item in a list or paragraph to create nested lists that maintain the original list's HTML attributes. In the Properties dialog box enter the type and style of the selected list or each of its elements.

1. Place the insertion point at the end of the word **statement**, third line of the numbered list, and press **Delete**.

2. Convert the last two lines of the text into independent paragraphs and, therefore, items of the numbered list. Press **Enter**, place the cursor at the end of the word **heating**, press **Delete** and click **Enter**. 🔲

3. With the editing cursor in the last item, press **Indent** in the **Properties** panel. 🔲

4. Indenting a list item creates a nested list with the original lists' HTML attributes. 🔲 The third item of the numbered list is now the first of the new nested list and is preceded by the number 1. Press the **Unordered List** option in the **Insert** panel.

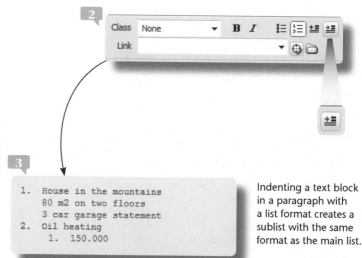

When you convert text lines in independent paragraphs, the new items are numbered consecutively.

Indenting a text block in a paragraph with a list format creates a sublist with the same format as the main list.

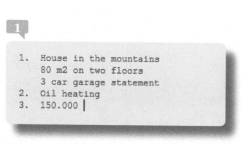

58

5. The number preceding the item disappears and gives way to a bullet point.  You now have an unordered list nested in the numbered list. Open the **Format** menu, click **List** and in the submenu select **Properties**.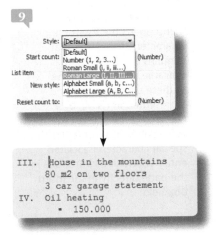

6. Define the appearance of the items in a list in the **List Properties** dialog box. In this case, the option **Bulleted List** is enabled in the **List type** drop-down menu. Display the **Style** box by clicking the arrow, select **Square** and **OK**.

7. The change affects the selected paragraph, the first and only item of the bullet list. Place the cursor at the beginning of the first word of the first item of the ordered list and click **List Item** in the **Properties** panel.

8. In the **List Properties** dialog box change the style of the numbered list to verify all items are affected by the change. Click the **Style** arrow dialog box and select **Roman Large**.

9. Enter the value **3** in the **Start count** field box and click **OK**.

10. Click the start of the second item of the numbered list and select **List Item**.

11. In the **List Item** section you can define a different property for each item. Click the arrow in the **New Style** field box, select **Roman Small** and click **OK** to finish.

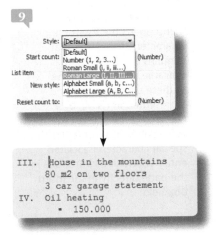

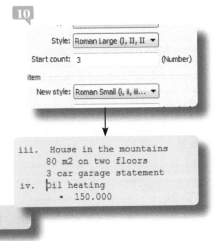

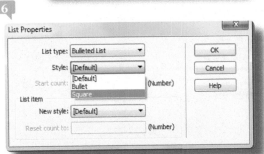

You can enter the value of the first item within the numbered list in the **Start count** field.

Inserting Special Characters

DREAMWEAVER'S DEFAULT SETTINGS ALLOW for one space between words. You can add additional spacing by inserting a non-breaking space character. To automatically add non-breaking spaces, select the Allow Multiple Consecutive Spaces in the Preferences dialog box.

1. Click with the edition cursor at the end of the fourth zero of the last page line, press the **space bar** twice and, after verifying that only one space is inserted, click **Preferences** in the **Edit** menu.

2. In the **General** category, select the **Allow multiple consecutive spaces** option and click **OK**.

3. Press the **space bar** and, after verifying the space is correctly inserted, open the **Insert** menu and display the **HTML** submenu.

4. Just as with line breaks, additional spaces are considered special characters. Display the **Special Characters** submenu and select **Non-Breaking Space**.

If the **Allow multiple consecutive spaces** option is disabled multiple spaces will be translated as being one sole space, since this is what browsers will do.

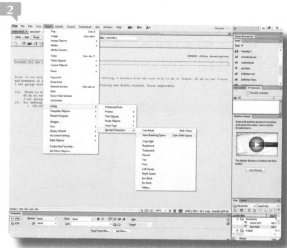

5. You can also specify special character preferences in the last option in the **Text** category of the **Insert** panel. Display this option and click the **Euro** option.

6. Save the changes and click the **index.htm** tab to expand the page.

7. Next, insert a horizontal rule between the second and third paragraph of the index.htm page. Horizontal rules are helpful for organizing information, separating texts and objects in a page. Click the first letter of the third paragraph, open the **Insert** menu, display the HTML submenu and select **Horizontal Rule**.

8. Once inserted, you can modify a horizontal rule. Enter the value **300** in the **W** (width) box in the **Properties** panel and press **Enter**.

9. By default, values are established in pixels but you can also indicate percentages, except for height settings, which can be expressed only in pixel fixed values. Enter the value **10** in the **H** (height) field box and press **Enter**.

10. Disable **Shading** by clicking the corresponding box.

11. Rules are, by default, center aligned, but you can align left or right by clicking your choice in the **Align** dialog box. The **Class** dialog box is for CSS styles. Save the changes made in the **index.htm** document to finish.

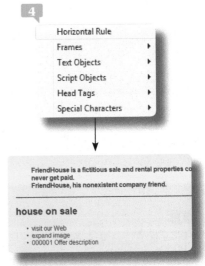

Use **Horizontal Rules** to organize information and to visually separate text and objects on a page.

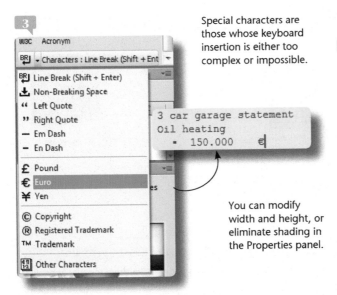

Special characters are those whose keyboard insertion is either too complex or impossible.

You can modify width and height, or eliminate shading in the Properties panel.

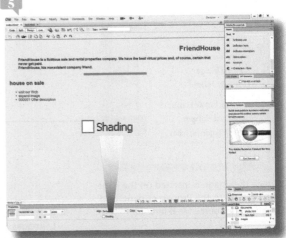

Inserting images

IMPORTANT

As the quality of a JPG file increases, so does the file size and file downloading time.

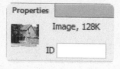

DREAMWEAVER SUPPORTS IMAGE FORMATS commonly used on the Internet. Among others, some of the formats offering good quality/size relation are GIF and PNG files. GIF (Graphic Interchange Format) files have up to 256 colors and maintain transparency. PNG (Portable Network Group), from Adobe Fireworks, supports indexed color, gray scale, and true-color images, and also supports alpha channels for transparency.

1. To complete the exercise, download, from our website, and copy the **house1.jpg** file to your document folder. Place the edition cursor at the end of the phrase **Price negotiable** in the **text.htm** page, and press **Enter**.

2. Select the **Common** category in the **Insert** panel, go to **Images** and select **Image**. 🔲

3. In the **Select Image Source** dialog box, locate the **house1.jpeg** file and press **OK**. 🔲

4. In the **Image Tag Accessibility Attributes** dialog box, click the **Change the Accessibility Preferences** link.

5. Disable the four options in the **Show attributes when inserting** section so that Dreamweaver doesn't ask for accessibility

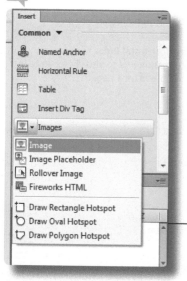

Once the image is inserted on the page, you can go to the Properties panel and modify the source file reference.

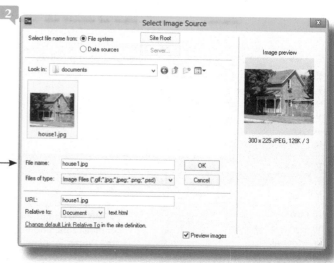

Images are one of the main elements on a page, make them visually appealing.

025

text when inserting attributes; press **OK** and click **Cancel** in the Attributes Preferences dialog box.

6. At the same time the image is being inserted at the point where the edition cursor was, the **Properties** panel shows you the size, width, and height. The file path of the original image appears later. Click the folder icon to the right of the **Src** field box in the **Properties** panel. **3**

7. The **Select Image Source** dialog box reopens so you can select another image file. Click the arrow of the **Relative to** field box and select **Site Root**. **4**

8. The document-relative path is very useful when the page and image referenced are in the same folder, but it can also be used to establish a link to a file image in the site's other folders. However, the root-relative path of a site indicates the path from the root folder to the image document. Click **OK** both in the Alert **5** and in the Selection dialog box.

9. If you eliminate the content in the **Src** field box, the document loses the image reference. Double-click in the **Properties** panel, and press **Delete** and **Enter**. **6**

10. Notice that the image doesn't upload correctly. Enter the following path in the box **/documents/house1.jpg** and press **Enter**. **7**

11. To change the reference to the image file so that it is relative to the **text.htm** document, enter two consecutive periods in the **Src** field box and press **Enter**.

The path of a relative reference begins with a slash (/), which represents a site's root folder.

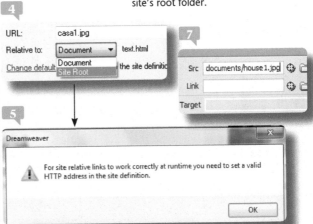

Sharing images

TO UPLOAD IMAGES, HTML pages use a reference to the source file that is contained in the site's folder. Creating a folder to store images avoids possible page reference loss problems. Dreamweaver lets you use the copy and paste functions for images contained in the page. The cut or copy of an image carries over the HTML reference established by the file's source directory.

IMPORTANT

The HTML reference of the image uploading page maintains the path relative to the image in relation to the page where it is uploaded.

1. The original image used in the page is contained in the documents site folder. In the **Files** panel click the boxed + next to the **documents** folder to view its contents. 🔲

2. Right-click **house1.jpg** and, in the **Edit** menu, select **Cut**. 🔲

3. Right-click the **images** folder, open the **Edit** menu and click **Paste**.

4. If the source document is deleted or its location changed, the page will not be able to upload the image. However, even so, the image remains uploaded on the page because its content has not yet been updated. Press **F5** to update files. 🔲

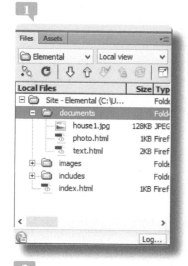

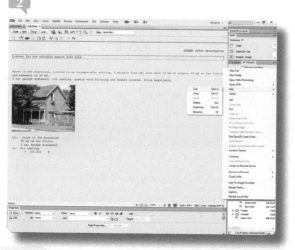

For correct uploading of the image, the source file should be located in the site's folders.

5. Next, practice copying images from different pages of the same site. Select images to be copied and click **Copy**. 🔲

6. Images can be pasted on one or more documents. In the **Files** panel, double-click the **photo.htm** page.

7. The page is in the **Elemental** site's **documents** folder, which is also the location of the **text.htm** page. Press the key combination **Ctrl + V** to paste the image. 🔲

8. Because **photo.htm** and **text.htm** are both located in the same site directory, the **documents** folder, the reference is the correct path for uploading the image. Expand the **index.htm** page.

9. The **index.htm** page is the **Elemental** site's main page and is, therefore, contained in the root folder. Place the cursor at the end of the third paragraph, after the word **sale**, and click **Paste** to insert the copied image.

10. Although the location has changed, the image is correctly uploaded because Dreamweaver automatically updates the source code inserting the new path in the field box. If this is not the case, 🔲 you need to either select or manually enter the path in the **Src** field. To finish, close and press **No** in the alert dialog box.

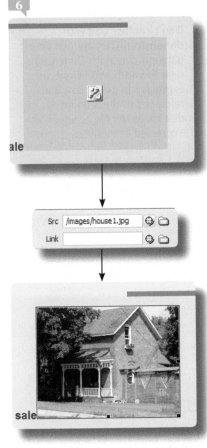

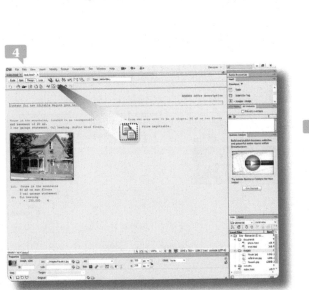

By default, the source reference is automatically updated.

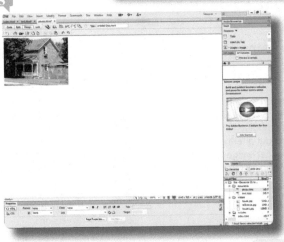

Resizing images

IMPORTANT

Don't confuse **size** with **dimension**. They are two very different concepts. Dimensions refer to width and height, as expressed in pixels; size is in reference to the amount of disk space the file occupies, as expressed in kilobytes.

TO RESIZE AN IMAGE drag the resizing handles or go to the Properties panel. To upload a resized image the user's browser scales it, increasing download time. To reduce download time and ensure that all instances of an image have the same size, you need to edit the original document. You can resize an image by reducing the image area and then resampling it. Resampling adds or subtracts pixels from a JPEG and GIF format previously resized to match the original image as much as possible.

1. The **Properties** panel displays the image's dimensions. In the **photo.htm** page, both page size and photo size coincide because the image is the only element in it. Select the image and enter the value **30** in the **W** field box and press **Enter.**

2. When width or height values are changed, two icons appear to the right of each of the **W** and **H** field boxes. The first icon reestablishes the original size of the image and the second icon, a new feature of this version, verifies that the changes have been made. Click the first icon to remove modifications.

3. Image resizing does not affect a file's size or kilobytes. Enter the value **400** in the **W** field box and press **Enter.**

The change in dimension affects the instance of the modified image only, without altering the original image file or the remaining file instances.

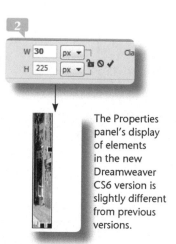

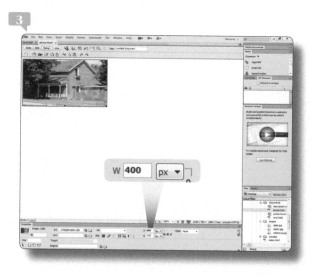

The Properties panel's display of elements in the new Dreamweaver CS6 version is slightly different from previous versions.

027

4. The user's browser scales the image when the page is loaded causing a delay in download time and poor browser image visualization. Enter the value **300** in the **H** field box and press **Enter**.

5. When you select an image, resize handles appear on the sides. Drag the handles to resize the image. Open the **Modify** menu, select **Image** and click **Crop**.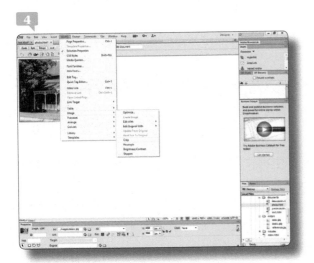

6. A dialog box alerts you that this action will permanently alter the image; click **OK**.

7. Corner handles can modify both dimensions at the same time, but central handles can change one dimension only. Click and drag one of them. To apply the changes press **Enter**.

8. Resized images loose sharpness. To solve this problem, click **Resample**, the fifth button in the **Edit** field of the **Properties** panel.

9. The program redistributes color information, adjusting the image to its new proportions. To verify that the resizing has affected all the instances in the **house1.jpg** file, open the **text.htm** page.

10. Insert the value **100** in the **W** field box and **75** in the **H** box, and press **Enter**.

11. To finish, go to the **File** menu and click **Save All**.

IMPORTANT

The small lock image icon to the right of the W and H fields in the Properties panel lets you restrict the proportions; by default, this function is disabled.

When you crop an image in Dreamweaver, the original file size and download time changes.

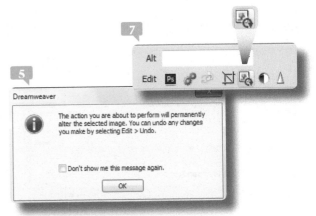

Enable the **Don't show me this message again** option, if you don't want the dialog box to appear when you edit the image

Image aligning

IMPORTANT

The **Top** option aligns the top part of the image with the top of the tallest element (image or text) in the current line. The **Text Top** option determines the alignment of the upper part of the image with the highest character text line.

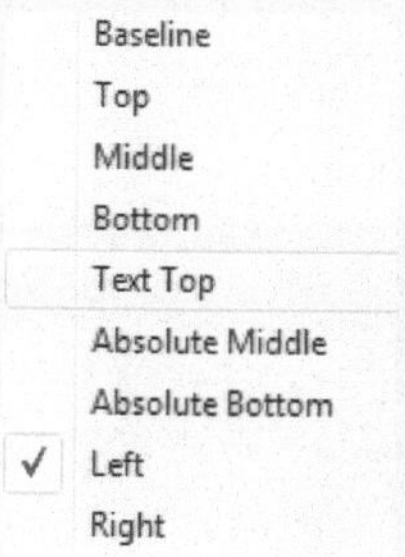

Baseline
Top
Middle
Bottom
Text Top
Absolute Middle
Absolute Bottom
Left
Right

BY DEFAULT IMAGES ARE DISPLAYED UNALIGNED, allowing the browser to set the corresponding parameters. In Dreamweaver CS6 you can modify the alignment of an image through the image's contextual menu. This new version has eliminated this function from the Properties panel. An image is aligned in relation to the other elements of the paragraph or line.

1. Start with an alternative text for the image on the **text.htm** page. Select the image and type the phrase **click to expand** in the **Alt** field box in the **Properties** panel, and press **Enter.** 1
2. Dreamweaver CS6 has also eliminated the **Border** option from the **Properties** panel, with which you could assign a border to an image, instead open the image in the default image editor and adjust accordingly. Images can be independently aligned in a page. To learn more about aligning an image use the **photo.htm** page that, for the moment, contains only one instance of the **house1.jpg** image file. Double-click the first word of the second paragraph.

When previewing the page, the Alternate Text appears when the cursor is over the image.

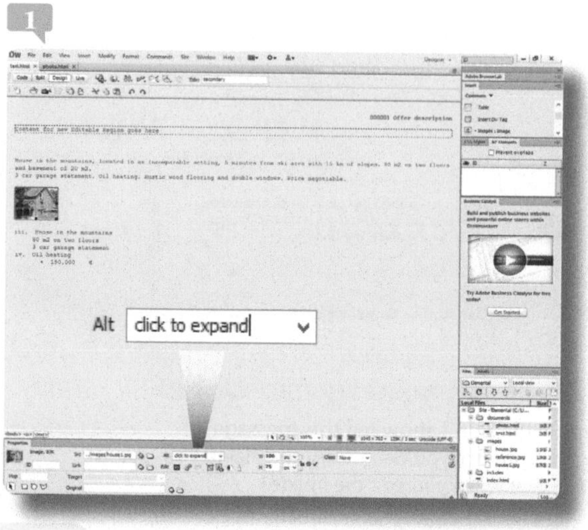

1
Alt
click to expand

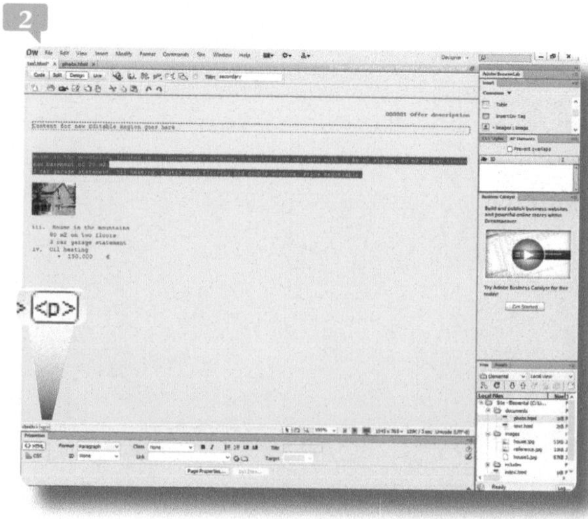

2
<p>

028

3. Click the **p** tag in the Status Bar, copy the selected text and expand **photo.htm**.

4. In an empty space on the page, to the right of the image, open the **Edit** menu and select **Paste Special**.

5. Select **Text only** in the **Paste Special** dialog box, and click **OK**.

6. The text is pasted without the format or original HTML attributes. Right-click the selected image, select **Align** and, in the submenu, click **Middle**.

7. The middle of the image is aligned with the baseline of the current line. Now go to the image's contextual menu and align it with the baseline.

8. The **Baseline** and **Bottom** aligns the text (or other element of the same paragraph) to the lower part of the selected object. Now, align left.

9. This action situates the selected image on the left margin, while the surrounding text is adjusted to the right margin. To finish, open the **File** menu and select **Save All**.

IMPORTANT

The Absolute Bottom option aligns the bottom part of the image with the bottom of the line of text (including descenders of certain characters). The Right align option places the image on the right margin of the page, adjusting the text to the left margin, and, the Absolute Middle, aligns the middle of the image with the middle of the current text line.

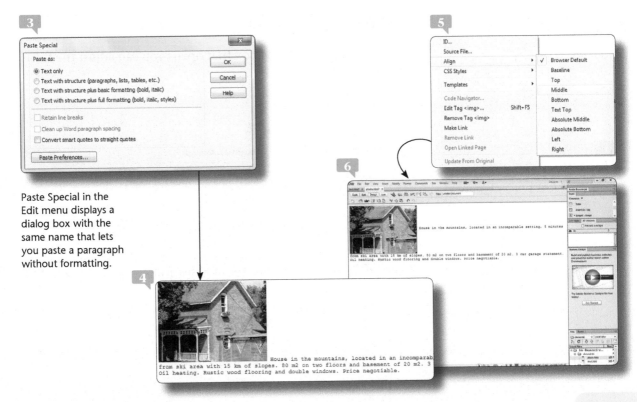

Paste Special in the Edit menu displays a dialog box with the same name that lets you paste a paragraph without formatting.

Knowing image editing features

DREAMWEAVER PROVIDES SEVERAL IMAGE EDITING FEATURES that when applied to a selected image also modifies the source image document. You will find these features under **Image** in **Modify,** or in the Property Inspector. The Brightness/Contrast feature corrects images that are either too dark or too light, and the Sharpness function adjusts the focus and defines the image.

1. Select the image, go to **Modify,** click **Image** and select **Brightness/Contrast.** **1**

2. This feature affects the highlights, shadows, and midtones of an image. The Brightness and Contrast values range from –100 to 100. Enter **10** in the **Brightness** field box and **20** in the **Contrast** box, and click **OK.** **2**

3. The changes made to the image affect the source document and, therefore, all the instances contained in the pages. The editing commands are displayed in the **Properties** panel in groups of buttons. Click **Sharpen,** the last command button in the **Edit** field. **3**

4. In the **Sharpen** dialog box that opens you can adjust the focus

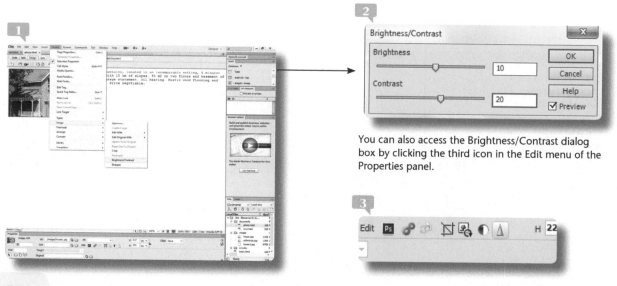

You can also access the Brightness/Contrast dialog box by clicking the third icon in the Edit menu of the Properties panel.

of an image by increasing the contrast around the edges. The values range from 0 to 10. Press **Cancel**.

5. Click on **Edit Image Settings**, the second icon in the **Edit** field.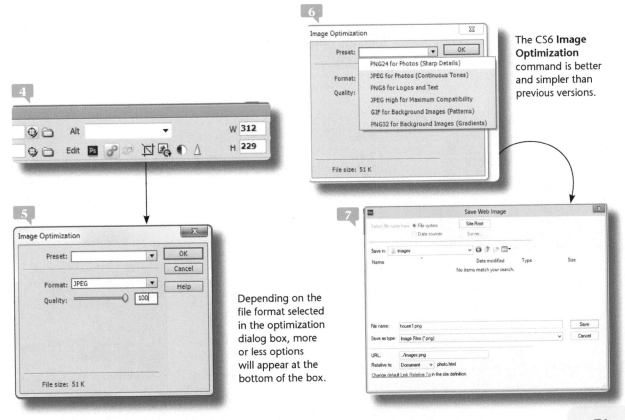

6. The options in the **Image Optimization** dialog box relate to the image file format that, in turn, can be changed in the **Format** drop-down menu options. Double-click the **Quality** box and enter the maximum value, **100**.

7. Use Image Optimization to achieve the best quality/size relation for an image. The **Preset** field lets you select an Image Optimization format that will be applied by default to all images. Open this field and select, for example, the **PNG24 for Photos (Sharp Details)**.

8. The **Format** field adjusts the options selected in **Preset**. Note that by clicking the **Help** button in this or any other dialog box you can obtain information relative to the enabled feature. Click **OK** and in the **Save Web Image** dialog box, find the site's image folder and press **Save**.

029

IMPORTANT

Note that the direct image editing options affect the source image. You can undo changes only before the page containing the instances is saved.

The CS6 **Image Optimization** command is better and simpler than previous versions.

Depending on the file format selected in the optimization dialog box, more or less options will appear at the bottom of the box.

Creating image maps and other adjustments

LARGE GRAPHIC FILES can be slow to download, which is why designers often use a two-bit version (black and white) of the main page that loads quickly for users to see until the larger image appears. This image, that disappears when the original image is loaded, is set in the Original field in the Properties panel. This same panel lets you create image maps, or images divided into regions called hotspots.

1. Download the **house1.psd** file containing the **house1.jpg** image converted to gray scale and saved in Photoshop format. Save the file to the **images** folder of the current site, update the **Files** panel and click the folder icon next to the **Original** field box in the **Properties** panel.

2. Select **house1.psd** in the **Select original File** window and click **OK**.

3. The **Image Optimization** dialog box appears at the same time the original file is displayed over the image. Maintain the default optimization options shown in the dialog box and click **OK**.

Don't confuse the Original field with the Source field.

030

4. To end this first part, go to the **Save Web Image** dialog box to store the image in jpeg format in the site's image folder.

5. In the second part of this exercise you will learn how to create image maps. An image map is an image that has been divided into regions called hotspots that when clicked an action occurs. Before you start, make sure the image is selected in the document window.

6. The Hotspot Tools are grouped in the bottom left-hand side of the Properties panel. By default the tool selected is the **Pointer**. Select the **Rectangle Hotspot** tool—the second one in the mentioned group.

7. Use the drag technique to use this tool. Draw a rectangle that includes the first floor window of the house in the image.

8. Drag the handles appearing in the hotspot area and modify image dimensions. The Properties panel updates automatically to set the hotspot area. You will use the hotspot area to establish links among pages and previewing documents. Click **Save** in the Standard toolbar.

In Dreamweaver, hotspots in pages are always visible to facilitate their selection and modification.

73

Inserting and updating PSD documents

IN DREAMWEAVER you can create Smart Objects from Photoshop images. Smart Objects are linked to the source file so that you can modify the original Photoshop image and update the Dreamweaver image without opening Photoshop.

1. Download the **house2.psd** sample file from our website and save it to the image folder. Place the cursor at the end of the **photo.htm** page and press **Enter** to create a new paragraph.

2. In the **Common** category of the **Insert** panel click **Image**.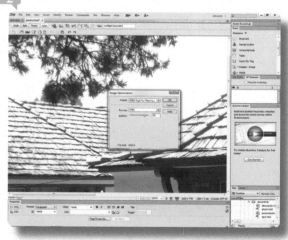

3. In the **Select Image Source** dialog box, open the **images** folder and select the **house2.psd** image and press **OK**.

4. The **Image Optimization** dialog box, where you can establish the format and quality of the image you want to publish on the web, appears on the screen. A new feature of this version is that the image is previewed directly on the active document. Maintain the default settings in the dialog box and click **OK**.

5. Store the web-ready image file to a location within the **Elemental** site's root folder. If the folder is not opened, find and open the site's **images** folder and click **Save**.

6. Dreamweaver creates Smart Objects based on the optimization settings established and places a web-ready version of the image on your page.  To resize the image go to the Properties panel and, in the **px** field box, change **px** to **5**, and enter the value **10** for both dimensions.

7. Observe the icons appearing in the upper left-hand corner of the image. Two green arrows tell you that the image is synchronized with the original image, while the alert symbol informs you that the dimensions don't coincide with those of the original image.  Select the image and press **Edit with Photoshop**, the first button next to **Edit** in the **Properties** panel.

8. The original image opens in Photoshop. To reduce the size by 10%, go to the **Reset Image Size** dialog box, in the **Image** menu.  Change from color mode to gray scale, save the changes made and close the Edit application.

9. For the changes made on the original image to be reflected on the copy, go to **Update from Original**, the third Edit button on the **Properties** panel.  To finish, save changes by pressing the key combination **Ctrl + S**.

IMPORTANT

You can also update a web-ready image that was modified by using the context's menu option **Update from Original**.

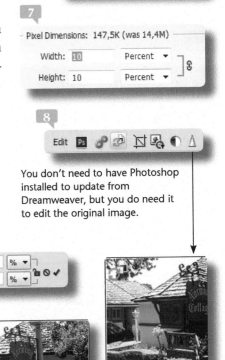

You don't need to have Photoshop installed to update from Dreamweaver, but you do need it to edit the original image.

Adding links

LINKS ARE FUNDAMENTAL COMPONENTS of a page that are used for navigation. They can be absolute or relative. Each web page has an exclusive address called a URL (Uniform Resource Locator). To link a document located on another server you need to use an absolute path with the complete URL address including the protocol of the linked document. Relative links are used for local links.

1. Open the main page of the **Elemental** site so that you can establish a series of links to other pages to browse within the site. In the **Files** panel double-click the **index.htm** page.

2. Create a local link for two documents on the site. Select the text **000001 Offer description** so that the link is associated with it.

3. Now, create hypertext that when clicked will take you to the linked file. There are several ways to insert a link. Open the **Modify** menu and click the **Make Link** command button.

4. In the **Select File** dialog box double-click the **documents** folder in the **Elemental** site.

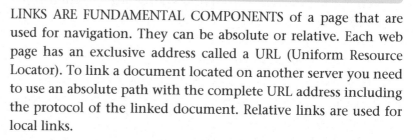

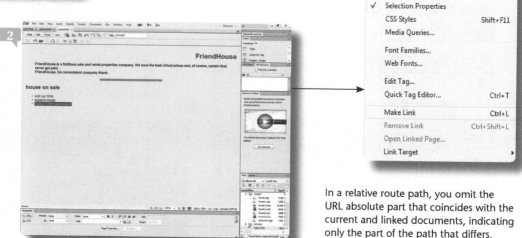

When a local link is created (links to documents in the same site) you don't need to specify the URL of the target document.

In a relative route path, you omit the URL absolute part that coincides with the current and linked documents, indicating only the part of the path that differs.

032

5. Link the selected text to the **text.htm** document. Select the **text.htm** page and click **OK**.

6. The selected text is automatically underlined to indicate a hypertext link. Select the **expand image** text and click the **Hyperlink** button, the first one in the **Common** category of the **Insert** panel.

7. The **Hyperlink** dialog box appears on the screen. The first reference is defined in the **Text** field where you can see the text displayed on the page. The **Link** field is related to the linked document. Press the folder icon to the right of this field and, in the **Select File** dialog box, double-click the **photo.htm** page.

8. Enter the document-relative path in the **Link** field. Once the link is established, click **OK**.

9. Practice inserting an absolute path. Select the text **visit our web**.

10. To link a document located on another server you need to use an absolute path with the document's full URL address and include the protocol to be used (usually http:// for web pages). Click the **Link** in the **Properties** panel, type the fake address, **http://www.friendhouse.com**, and click **Enter**.

11. To finish the exercise click **Save** in the Standard toolbar to store the changes.

IMPORTANT

Although you can also use absolute paths for local links, it is not recommended, if you move the site to another domain the local absolute path links will break.

You can type the relative or absolute route of the target document directly in the **Link** box.

The **protocol** indicates the mode in which the connection and transfer of information is made among the different systems.

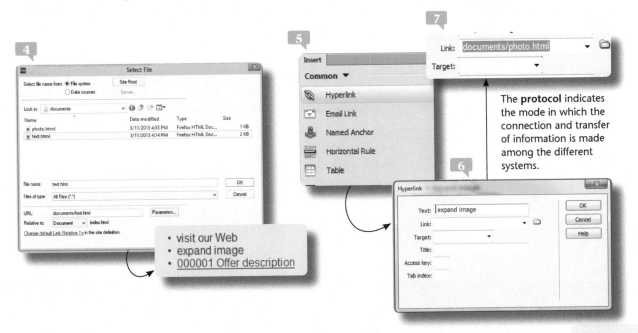

- visit our Web
- expand image
- 000001 Offer description

Troubleshooting navigation errors

THE DESIGNER OF A SITE needs to determine the target audience and browsers for his or her site. Dreamweaver helps you check for errors generated in browsers. The program discriminates among three types of problems, of different level of importance, in page codification: errors, warnings, and information messages. Dreamweaver provides a report generator that identifies problems related to CSS in browsers without having to execute them, saving time and guaranteeing a more stable experience between browsers and operative systems.

1. With the **index.htm** page active, click the **Check browser compatibility** button.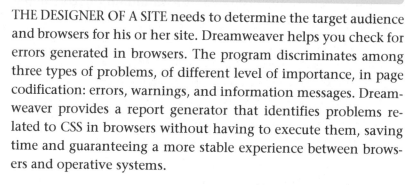

2. This feature includes all the options related to page and browser compatibility. Select **Settings**.

3. In the **Target Browsers** dialog box you can establish the browsers to be checked. Although all browsers accept the usual page elements, others are admitted only by some. To facilitate the functioning of your website, keep all the browsers and versions active. Press **OK**.

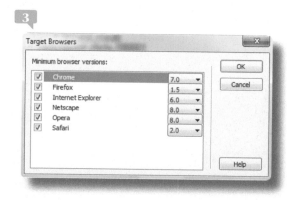

4. This action opens a new group of panels showing the **Browser Compatibility** content. The left section of the panel displays the errors that have been detected, as well as the code line where they are located. In this case, as you can see, no errors have been detected. 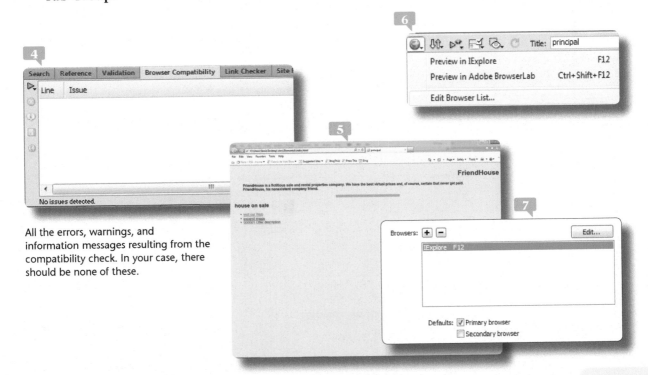 The program previews the pages in different browsers. Internet Explorer is the default browser to preview pages. Open the **File** menu and select **Preview in Browser** to choose your browser.

5. The page is visualized correctly. Close the browser and, back in Dreamweaver, click the command represented by a globe in the **Document Bar** and select **Edit Browser List**.

6. The program allows for the use of alternative browsers. Go to the category **Preview in Browser** in the **Preferences** dialog box to set preferences. **Internet Explorer** is the default browser for previewing. If you have another browser installed on your computer select it and make it your secondary option by clicking the **Secondary browser** option. Internet Explorer remains as the main browser and can be activated by clicking the key that enables page preview, key F12. Click the **OK** button to apply the selected settings and, last, click the Option icon in the **Browser Compatibility** panel and select **Close Tab Group**.

033

IMPORTANT

Errors are marked with a red exclamation point, **warnings** with a yellow exclamation point. A text globe icon displays the **information messages**.

All the errors, warnings, and information messages resulting from the compatibility check. In your case, there should be none of these.

Previewing pages

DREAMWEAVER LETS YOU PREVIEW THE PAGES you are editing to verify they are being correctly displayed on the browser. By default, pages are previewed in Internet Explorer, the established main browser, but you can also preview pages in other browsers you may have installed in your computer. Previews also help verify if page links are functioning correctly. A new feature of the CS6 version is the multiscreen preview option that allows previewing pages in different size screens, according to the device used for displaying.

1. Go to **Preview/Debug in browser** in the **Documents** Bar and select **Preview in IExplorer** to see the main page of the **index.htm** website.

2. The page is automatically uploaded in the browser. Verify that the links function correctly. Click the link **000001 Offer description.**

3. The link functions correctly and the page is uploaded to the browser. Go back to the previous page and click on the link to expand the image.

The function key F12 activates previewing of the page in the main browser.

4. It appears that all your links function correctly. Close the browser to return to Dreamweaver.

5. The second part of the exercise is about multiscreen previewing, the new Dreamweaver CS6 feature. To start, open the **photo.htm** document.

6. Display the **File** menu and click the new **Multiscreen Preview** command button.

7. The **Multiscreen Preview** window is divided into three parts that correspond to a device screen type, phone, tablet, and desktop; dimensions are set in parentheses next to each screen name. As simple as this, you can now preview and see your site in different target screens. Use the screen's scroll bar to see all the page's contents.

8. The **Media Queries** command button lets you specify different CSS files for each device without affecting their compatibility. The **Viewport Sizes** command button is for specifying different sizes for each screen.

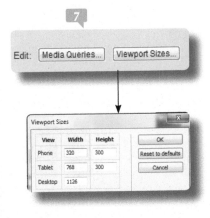

Modifying link properties

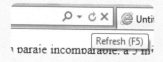
IN DREAMWEAVER YOU CAN CHOOSE WHAT COLORS TO APPLY TO LINKS depending on their status, normal, visited, or active. You can modify a file's default colors in the Properties dialog box of the page in question. The color chart in the Appearance category of the page's Property dialog box allows you to match color with link status, meaning that, as long as you are not using CSS styles, you can associate a link status (normal, visited, active) with a specific color.

1. Start practicing on the **index.htm** page. Go to the Properties panel and click **Page Properties.**

2. Activate the **Appearance (HTML)** category and click the arrow point in the **Links** color box.

3. The color you select from the chart is the color in which links that have not been visited will appear when the page is uploaded in the browser for the first time. Select the color red.

4. You can also select a color for visited links. Click the arrow point in the **Visited links** field, and select an intense blue.

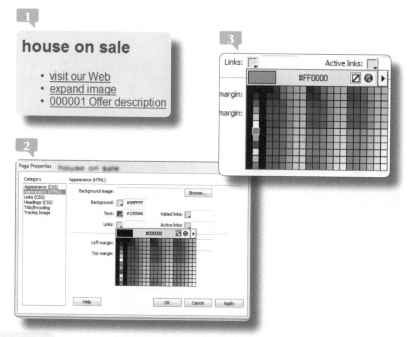

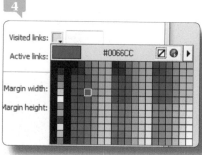

You can select a color from the chart by clicking your preference or do so manually by entering the color combination of your choice in the fields for that purpose.

035

5. You can also select colors for active links, meaning those that were last used. Click the arrow point in the **Active links** field and select maroon. **5**

6. Remember that because you are not using CSS styles, the options for defining page properties are limited to those aspects that can be specified through HTML tags. Click **OK**.

7. Verify that the color applied to links is correct. In Dreamweaver, all normal links, meaning links not visited or active, will appear in the specified red color. **6** Save changes and press **F12**.

8. Blue color links are those you visited when completing previous exercises. **7** Click the **expand image** link.

9. The page uploads correctly. Go back to the previous page and verify that the color of the active links is maroon. **8**

10. The Dreamweaver **Appearance (HTML)** category in the **Page Properties** dialog box allows link color definition according to three link types. To finish the exercise, close the web browser to return to Dreamweaver.

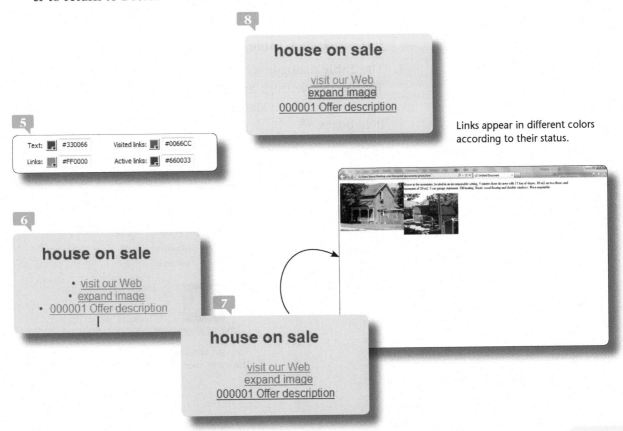

Links appear in different colors according to their status.

Inserting tables

TABLES ARE VERY EFFECTIVE TOOLS for presenting data and establishing a layout for HTML pages. A table consists of one or more rows made up of one or more cells distributed in columns. Dreamweaver provides two ways of visualizing and creating tables: the standard mode in which charts are presented in a grid-like form of rows and columns or the design mode that allows you to draw your own table.

1. Go to the **Files** panel, click the arrow in the **Show** drop-down menu and select the **styles** site.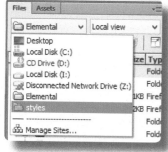

2. The **styles** site has one page only, in its higher level, **index.htm** that was established as the site's main page. The other site pages are stored in the **documents** folder. Press the boxed + to the left of the documents folder to find the **text.htm** page and double-click it to open it.

3. In this exercise you will learn how to insert tables. In the **Insert** panel, click **Table**.

4. The **Table** dialog box, where you can specify settings, opens. The default settings are tables of three rows and three columns. Enter the value 4 in both the **Rows** and **Columns** field boxes.

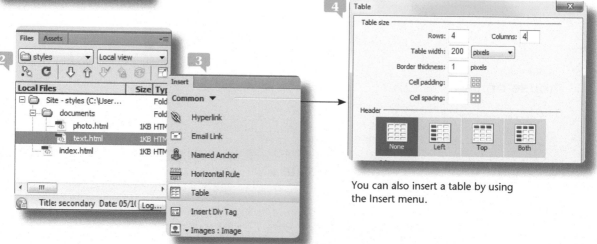

You can also insert a table by using the Insert menu.

036

5. Enter the value **400** in the **Table width** field box and delete the value in the **Border thickness** box.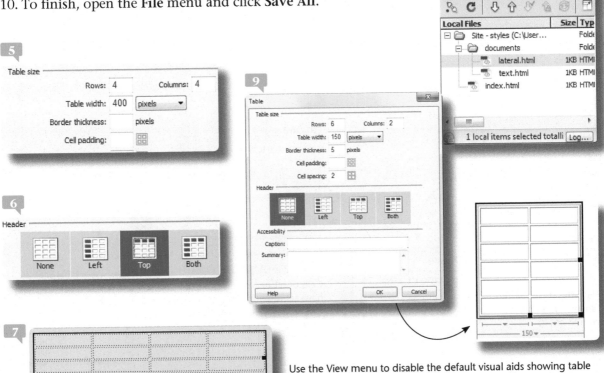

6. The next two options in the dialog box are **Cell padding**, which defines space in relation to the cell and its contents, and **Cell spacing**, which defines space in relation to other adjacent cells. Select **Top** in the **Header** section so that the first row cells appear in a different format than the rest and click **OK**.

7. A table with the specified characteristics is inserted in the page automatically. Insert a second table in the **photo.htm** document. But first, go to the **Files** panel to rename the page as **lateral.htm** and click the Enter key to confirm the page name and click Enter again to open the document.

8. Press the **Table** option in the **Common** category in the **Insert** panel.

9. Following the above instructions, create a table of **6 rows** and **2 columns**, a **width of 150 pixel**, **5 pixel border thickness**, **2 pixel cell spacing**, and no header.

10. To finish, open the **File** menu and click **Save All**.

IMPORTANT

If you don't specify a border thickness value, most browsers display tables using the set value of 1 pixel. To ensure browsers display tables with no borders, set border value thickness to 0 pixels.

Use the View menu to disable the default visual aids showing table width and border thickness when inserting tables.

Working with rows, columns and cells

THE NUMBER OF ROWS AND COLUMNS IN A TABLE is defined in the Table dialog box, but you can also add or delete at your convenience with the help of visual aids. Once the row or column is selected you can access the options in the Table submenu of the Modify menu or press Delete if what you want is to eliminate a row(s) or column(s). You can also add multiple rows or columns by opening the Insert Rows or Columns dialog box in the mentioned submenu. Note that cells adjust to accommodate content.

1. Click inside the first cell of the table contained in the **lateral.htm** page, enter the word **home** and click the first cell in the second row.

2. The width of the columns automatically adjusts to the content inserted in the first cell. Type the word **properties** and click the second cell in the third row.

3. Type the word **sale** and click the second cell, fourth row.

4. Type the word **rent** and click the first cell, fifth row.

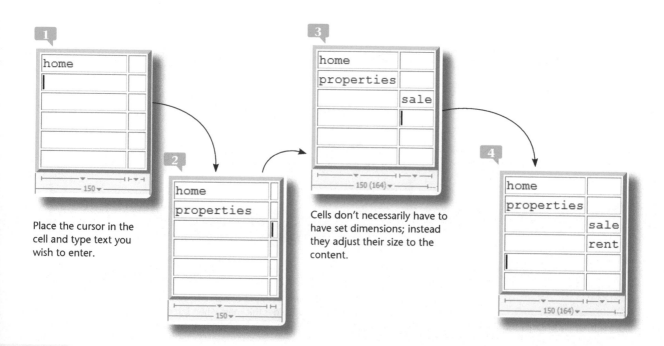

Place the cursor in the cell and type text you wish to enter.

Cells don't necessarily have to have set dimensions; instead they adjust their size to the content.

037

5. Type the word **contact** and click the next cell.

6. The selection is highlighted in red when the pointer is positioned on the left edge of the first cell. Position the pointer on the left edge of the row and click when cells are highlighted in red.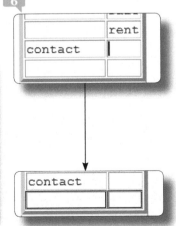

7. Open the **Modify** menu, click the **Table** option and select **Delete Row**.

8. Click the top edge of the table on the second column header, display the **Modify** menu, go to the **Table** submenu and select **Insert Column**.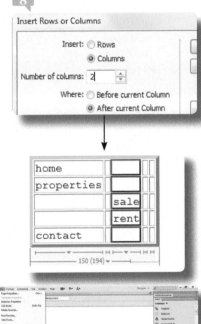

9. A new column, preceding the selected column, appears. The same follows when adding a row. The added row precedes the selected row. Open the **Modify** menu, click **Table** and select **Insert Rows or Columns**.

10. In the **Insert Rows or Columns** dialog box click **Columns**, enter the value 2 in the **Number of columns** field box and click **OK**.

11. Each column has a visual aid in the shape of an arrow point. Click the visual aid below the second to last column and click **Select Column** in the menu appearing on the screen.

12. To select two columns at the same time click the top edge of the table on the last column header while pressing the **Ctrl** key.

13. Press the **Delete** key to eliminate the two columns selected. To finish, press key combination **Ctrl + S**.

IMPORTANT

The value entered in the **Number of** field box specifies the number of rows or columns in a table. You can add either new rows or new columns but not both elements at the same time.

Modifying table properties

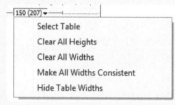
YOU CAN USE THE PROPERTIES PANEL TO EDIT TABLE PROPERTIES such as the margins of the text or content of the cell in relation to its borders, alignment or thickness of internal borders, among others. Other properties, such as background or border color, can be established using the corresponding page code.

1. Select the table and enter the value **5** in the **CellPad** field box in the **Properties** panel and click **Enter.**

2. Enter the same value, **5**, in the **CellSpace** field box and click **Enter.**

3. Click the arrow in **Align** and select **Center.**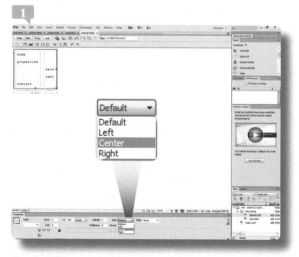

4. Now try modifying the background and border color. Click **Split** in the Document toolbar so that it also shows the page code.

5. By default the table color is the same as the page's background color. To change, you need to enter the corresponding table property in the code. Click the end of line 9 before the closing angular parenthesis and press the space bar.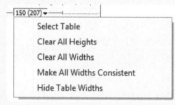

6. A list of properties appears. Double-click **bgcolor**, the option that corresponds to the background color characteristic.

To select the entire table structure, click the table's upper-left corner.

038

7. Choose, for example, a light green in the color sample chart appearing on the screen and in the **Properties** panel click **Refresh** to view the effect.

8. You can also change the table's border color. Press the space bar and click **border color** in the list that appears.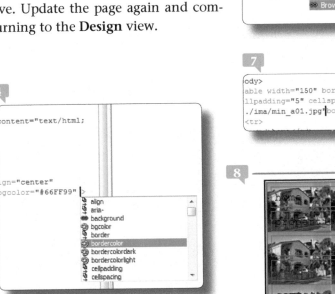

9. Select a darker green from the chart and press **Refresh**.

10. You can also insert a background image for the table, which should be stored in the site's folder. Go to the **styles** site in the **Files** panel and create a new folder with the name **ima**, go to our download site and paste files **gra_a01.jpg**, **gra_v01.jpg**, **min_a01.jpg**, and **min_v01.jpg**.

11. Use one of these files as the background. Select **bgcolor=** and the code of the selected color and click **Delete**.

12. Press the space bar, select **background**  and click the **Browse** button that appears on the screen.

13. In the **Select File** dialog box double-click the **ima** folder, select the **min_a01** file and click **OK**.

14. Confirm the code change 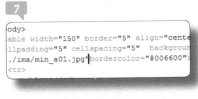 and refresh.

15. The background image is reproduced in mosaic format and the visualization of the cell's content is incorrect.  Delete the background characteristic from the code and reapply the light green color as above. Update the page again and complete the exercise by returning to the **Design** view.

The corresponding alphanumeric combination appears in code when selecting the background or border color.

Editing rows, columns and cells

IMPORTANT

When applying a CSS format to text from the Properties panel, Dreamweaver incorporates the new properties in the header section of the page or in an independent style sheet.

DREAMWEAVER LETS YOU SPECIFY PROPERTIES for a table or for selected rows, columns, and cells. Cell formatting takes precedence over row and column formatting, and even takes precedence over formatting for the entire table. When you select a row, column, or cell, the Properties panel displays the characteristics and options of the selected element, such as Horz (horizontal) and Vert (vertical), that aligns content in relation the row, column, or cell, No Wrap to prevent line wrapping, and Headers, to format selected cells as table headers.

1. Practice on the **lateral.htm** document. Click the upper edge of the first column.

2. Modify the column's text properties using CSS format, which will be explained in more detail later. Press the **CSS** button in the **Properties** panel, display the menu in the **Targeted Rule** field and select **New In-Line Style.**

3. Open the **Font** field on the **Properties** panel and select the **Arial, Helvetica, sans-serif** combination.

4. The format modifications made to cell content affects the columns and the table, adjusting dimensions accordingly. Row and column formatting takes precedence over table format-

To select a column, click its upper border and to select a row, click its left border.

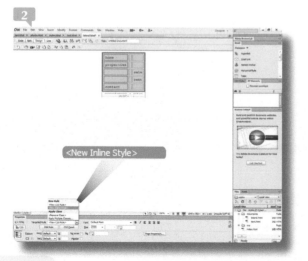

CSS styles reduce file size and provide designers with better control over their designs.

039

ting and cell formatting takes precedence over row and column formatting. Because modifying cell properties affects the content of all of the selected cells, selecting rows and columns makes it easier to assign attributes to the cell selected. Click the **HTML** button in the **Properties** panel.

5. In the lower section of the panel are the options for rows or, as in this case, columns. Click the **Horz** field arrow button and select **Center** to horizontally align the content of the rows or columns.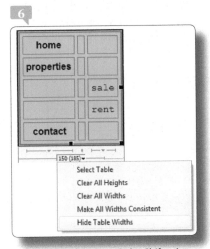

6. The **W** and **H** field boxes display width and height of the selected cells in pixels. The cells resize to adjust to content. The **No wrap** option prevents the text from wrapping, keeping all the text contained in the cell on one single line. Enable the **Header** option. 5

7. The **Header** option applies header formatting to the selected cells. To disable the visual aids in reference to widths, press the arrow point of any one of the visual aids and select **Hide Table Widths.** 6

8. Select the third row of the table by clicking its left border. Place the pointer on the left border of the next row and, while pressing the **Ctrl key**, click it. 7

9. Activate the panel's **CSS** properties. Enable the option **New InLine Style** in the **Targeted Rule field** and, in the **Font** field, select **Arial, Helvetica, sans-serif**.

10. Finish the exercise by clicking **Save** to store the changes made in the **lateral.htm** document.

Press key combination Ctrl + Shift + I to hide all visual aids.

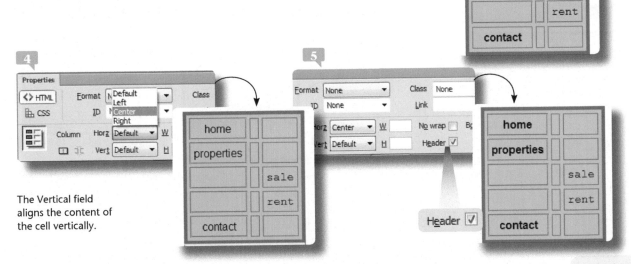

The Vertical field aligns the content of the cell vertically.

Splitting and merging cells

IN DREAMWEAVER YOU CAN MERGE ADJACENT CELLS to form one single cell containing the initial content and format. You can use the Menu Bar or the Properties panel for this task. When you click inside a cell you activate the edition cursor. To select the cell in question, click while pressing the Ctrl key. Dreamweaver also lets you split cells, making new ones in the selected row or column. You can set the preferences in the Split dialog box.

1. Click to the left of the first row, go to **Modify** menu, select **Table** and, in the submenu, click **Merge Cells.**

2. The first row is now made up of one single cell occupying the total width of the table. The content, the word **home**, and the format attributed to the cells in the first row in the previous exercise, remains unaltered. Click the left border of the last row.

3. You can also merge cells by using the **Properties** panel. When available, the **Merge Cells** option, the first option in the lower section of the panel, is activated. Click it.

4. Add a new row before learning to split a cell instead of merging. Open the **Modify** menu, display the **Table** submenu and select **Insert Row**.

Use the key combination
Ctrl + Alt + M to merge cells automatically.

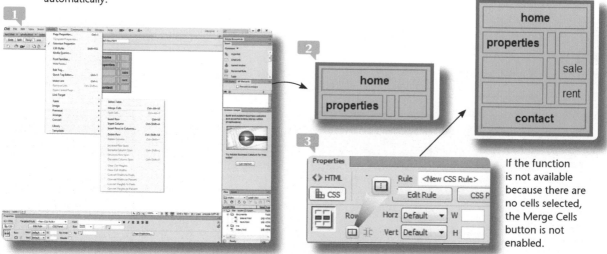

If the function is not available because there are no cells selected, the Merge Cells button is not enabled.

040

5. The inserted row has the same format as the selected row. You can split a cell in several rows or columns, even if they have been originally merged. Select a new row.

6. You can activate the Split option by using the **Table** submenu in the **Modify** menu or by clicking the **Split Cells** option next to the **Merge Cells** command in the **Properties** panel. 4

7. Open the **Split Cells** dialog box to choose where you want the split cells to appear, below or to the right of the selection. The default **Columns** option is set to a horizontal cell insertion. Enter the value **2** in the **Number of columns** field and click **OK**. 5

8. The selected row now has two cells. 6 Press **Delete** to eliminate the row.

9. Click the first cell of the second row while keeping the **Ctrl** key pressed. 7

10. In the Standard toolbar, select **Cut**, 8 click inside the first cell of the next row and click **Paste**.

11. Pasted cells retain the format and content of the cut cells. 9 Click the second cell of the second to last row while pressing the **Shift** key; next press the Merge Cells button in the **Properties** panel. 10

12. Click the left border of the second row to select it and click **Delete**.

13. To save the changes press the key combination **Ctrl + S** and click the Close button of the **lateral.htm** page to finish.

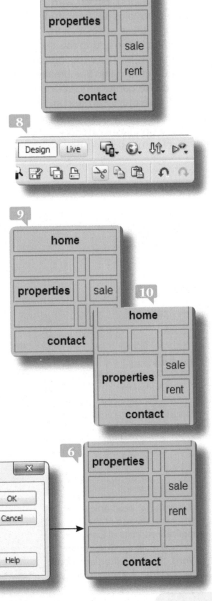

You can access the Split Cells dialog box by pressing the key combination Ctrl + Alt + S.

Using Excel and Word with Dreamweaver

DREAMWEAVER LETS YOU INSERT WORD OR EXCEL generated content. In the Design View Preferences dialog box you can choose how to insert the content in your web page. Similar to .doc or .docx files (Word), Excel files can be imported, although they can sometimes lose their formatting. To preserve the formatting use the Paste Special function in the Edit menu.

1. Click the top left corner of the table in the **text.htm** page. (Remember you are working in the **styles** site.)

2. By default, Dreamweaver pastes text with basic structure, meaning paragraphs and tables, in HTML format. To complete this exercise, copy the Word document **rent.doc** and the Excel file **sale.xls** from our download site. After you've copied and saved the documents to the site folder, go to the **Files** panel, select that same folder and open **rent.doc**.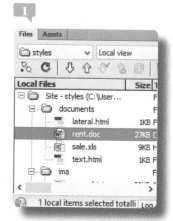

3. The document contains a Word-generated table. Click the top left corner to select and click the **Copy** command in the **Clipboard** tool option  and exit using the close button in the Title Bar.

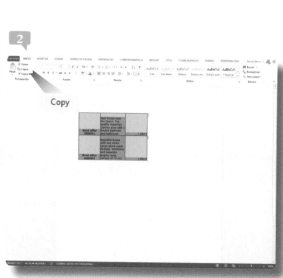

Copy

Microsoft has been able to generalize the use of the applications in its office suites. The two main applications are **Word**, the text editor, and **Excel**, the calculus worksheet manager.

The shortcut, Ctrl + V, or the Paste command, implies the Paste Text application without the table format.

4. Open the **Edit** menu and select **Paste Special**.

5. Select the fourth option in the **Paste Special** dialog box and click **OK**.

6. The table is pasted onto Dreamweaver in the original format. Click **Save** in the **Standard** toolbar.

7. Place the cursor at the beginning of the page, go to the **Files** panel to locate **sale.xls** and double-click it to open.

8. The document is uploaded. Excel worksheets are organized as tables, in rows and columns. Hold the **Shift** key and click cell **C2**.

9. Click **Copy** in the **Clipboard** to copy the selected cells.

10. Keep the Excel program open to ensure the paste function is correctly applied; otherwise the text without the format will be pasted. Return to Dreamweaver, open the **Edit** menu and select **Paste Special**.

11. In the **Paste Special** dialog box, verify that the fourth option is selected and click **OK**.

12. There are now two tables in the **text.htm** page, one Word and one Excel. Press **Enter** to separate them.

13. Last, click the **Horizontal Rule** command in the Common category of the **Insert** panel to insert the mentioned element between both tables.

IMPORTANT

Remember that once inserted on the page, you can change the **Horizontal rule** properties by using the Properties panel.

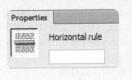

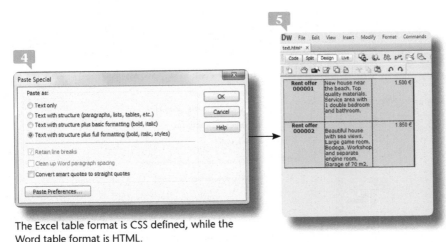

The Excel table format is CSS defined, while the Word table format is HTML.

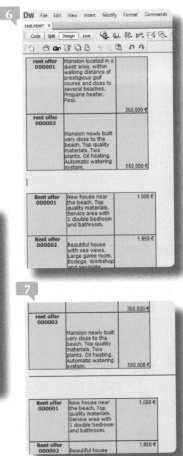

Clearing HTML code

DREAMWEAVER LETS YOU REMOVE UNNECESSARY HTML code. Select your preferences in the Clean Up HTML/XHTML dialog box to clean up HTML code. The removal of empty or redundant combination tags improves incorrect or illegible HTML codes. The program also has a specific dialog box for HTML codes obtained from Microsoft Office. The Commands menu provides access to dialog boxes that display a log of cleanup actions made.

1. Dreamweaver allows for the automatic deletion of unnecessary HTML code generated while editing documents. Open the **Commands** menu and click **Clean Up XHTML.**

2. Go to the **Clean Up HTML/XHTML** dialog box and select settings for the code cleanup process. The **Remove** option allows you to select different types of deleted codes. The **Empty container tags** option removes tags with no content. The **Redundant nested tags** option eliminates redundant instances of tags. Click the **Non-Dreamweaver HTML comments** option verification box.

3. Leave the other two unselected since they refer to advanced actions related to the use of templates and deletion of specific

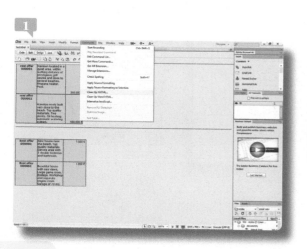

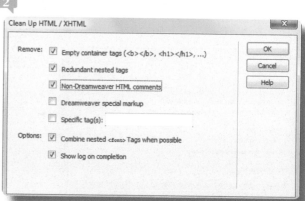

The Non-Dreamweaver HTML Comments function deletes the comments of codes originating from other programs.

code tags to be defined. The first option in the **Options** menu refers to the combination of different tags that control text formatting, if the option is available. Click **OK**.

4. The program doesn't detect any specific tags. Click **OK** in the dialog box.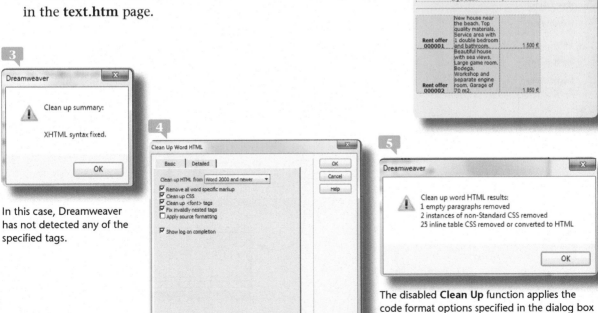

5. Dreamweaver provides a command that allows cleaning of HTML codes generated by Office applications. Go to the **Commands** menu and select **Clean Up Word HTML**.

6. The option **Remove all word specific markup** removes Word-specific HTML codes. **Clean up CSS** removes Word-specific CSS codes and CSS style attributes from tables and all unused style definitions. The following two options, **Clean up <font> tags** and **Fix invalidly nested tags**, activate the elimination of font tags inserted by Word. Disable **Apply source formatting** and click **OK** to clear.

7. In the dialog box showing the cleanup results, click **OK**.

8. The cleanup action has eliminated the CSS styles and left the Excel table with its predetermined format. But the Word generated table was automatically converted to HTML when it was inserted in the page. The cell properties not affected by the cleanup are HTML-defined tags generated by Dreamweaver. Click **Save** in the **Standard** toolbar to store changes made in the **text.htm** page.

In this case, Dreamweaver has not detected any of the specified tags.

The disabled **Clean Up** function applies the code format options specified in the dialog box **Program preferences**.

Nesting tables

IN DREAMWEAVER YOU CAN NEST TABLES, that is, insert a table of different levels inside another table. To nest a table, place the edit cursor inside a given cell of the main table and proceed as you would normally. Note that the width of the nested table cannot be wider than the main table.

1. The **text.htm** document already has two tables. Insert a third table that will function as the main table. Go to the **Insert** panel and click **Table**.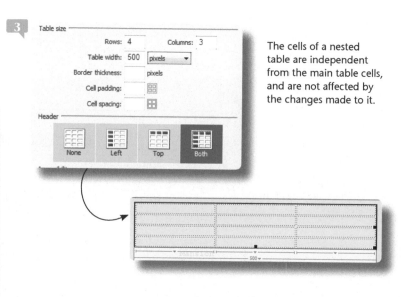

2. Insert the number of rows and columns of the new table. Enter the value **4** in the **Rows** field box and **3** in the **Columns** box, and **500** pixels for the width.

3. Delete the **Border thickness** and **Cell spacing** values.

4. Set a header format for the top cell row and the first column of cells. Select **Both** in the **Header** menu and click **OK**.

5. Click inside the first cell of the newly inserted table and in the **Insert** panel click **Table**.

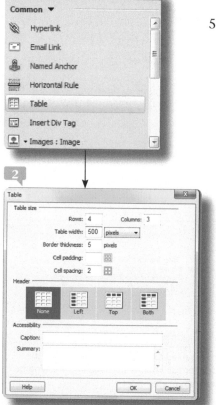

The cells of a nested table are independent from the main table cells, and are not affected by the changes made to it.

98

6. Click **OK** without changing any values.

7. A new table is inserted in the first cell of the main table. Click **Delete** to eliminate the nested table.

8. Select the table located in the center of the page and click **Cut** in the Standard toolbar.

9. Click the last cell in the second row of the table at the top of the page and click **Paste**.

10. The container cell adjusts its dimensions to the new content.  Select the horizontal rule located between the tables and press **Cut** again; place the cursor inside the last cell of the third row of the table at the top of the page and click **Paste**.

11. Select the table at the bottom of the screen, press **Cut**, click inside the last cell and click **Paste**.

12. Select the table you just pasted inside the last cell of the main table.

13. The selected nested table's **table** tag, displayed in the Status Bar, is included inside the main table's <table> tag. 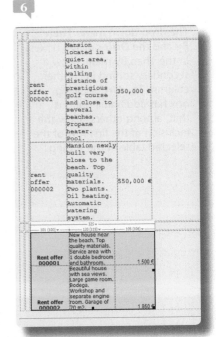 Go to the **Align** menu in the Properties panel and select **Center**. Do the same for the table in the second row of the main table.

14. To finish, select the first row of the main table, press **Merge Cells** in the Properties panel and click the key combination **Ctrl + S** to store the changes.

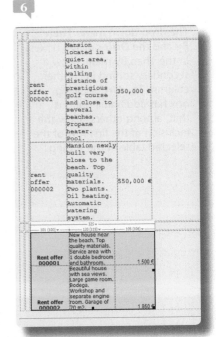

<body> <table> <tr> <td> <table> <tr>

You can verify how the nested table's tags are positioned in the page's Standard Status Bars.

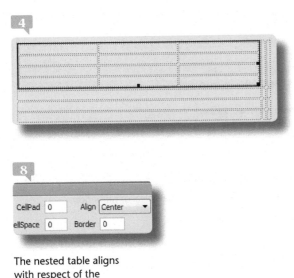

| CellPad | 0 | Align | Center ▼ |
| ellSpace | 0 | Border | 0 |

The nested table aligns with respect of the container cell.

The width of the nested table is limited by the width of the main table.

Sorting tables

DREAMWEAVER HAS A TABLE ROW SORTING FUNCTION based on the content of a single column and a more advanced function for two columns. You cannot sort tables containing merged cells or table headers. Set your sorting options in the Sort Table dialog box in the Commands menu. The Sort By dialog box specifies the column values to be used for sorting table rows, while the Order dialog box specifies how to sort, alphabetically or numerically, ascending or descending order.

1. Select the first nested table in the main table. Go to the **Commands** menu and click **Sort Table**. 〔1〕

2. The **Sort Table** dialog box opens. The **Sort By** menu specifies the column's values to be used for sorting rows. The **Order** field specifies the order criteria. Go to the **Order** menu and change **Ascending**, the default value, to **Descending**. The **Then By** option is a more advanced function that sorts tables based on the content of two columns. Go to **Options** and enable **Sort includes the first row** and click **OK**. 〔2〕

IMPORTANT

The drop-down menu **Then By** and the **Order** dialog boxes in the Then By menu allow a secondary sorting in another column. The **Order** dialog box has additional options that, among others, allow the inclusion of the first row of the selected table in the sorting.

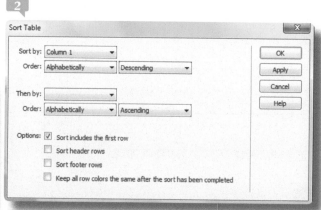

The established order can be alphabetical or numerical, descending or ascending.

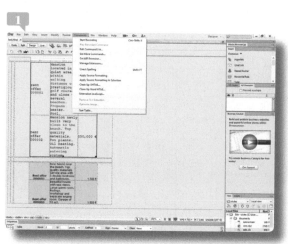

Sorting is not possible in merged tables or with different row and column dimensions.

3. Sorting is done according to the established settings. The order of the first column of the table has been specified as being alphabetically descending. The rest of the columns readjust accordingly. Click the first cell of the selected nested table and, while pressing the **Ctrl** key, click the same cell.

4. Press and hold down the **Ctrl** key while clicking the first cell in the next row to include it in the sort.

5. Only the headers application can modify the sorting functions. Click **Bold** in the **Properties** panel, HTML View.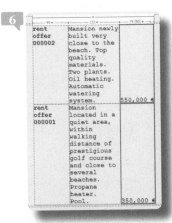

6. Click the arrow button in the **Vert** dialog box and select **Top**.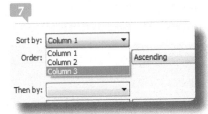

7. Now try a secondary sorting using the last column of the nested table. Click the top border of the last column to select all the cells.

8. Click the arrow in the **Vert** dialog box in the **Properties** panel and select **Bottom**.

9. Go to **Commands** and select **Sort Table**.

10. Select the column determining the sorting. Click the arrow in **Sort By** and select **Column 3**.

11. Click the arrow in **Alphabetically** and select **Numerically**.

12. Click the verification box in **Sort includes the first row**, click **OK**, deselect the table and save the changes.

044

IMPORTANT

By default the program excludes the sorting of the first row because it is generally used as a table header. It also excludes cells with a header format.

It is not necessary that a table is completely selected to sort it, as long as one of its elements is selected.

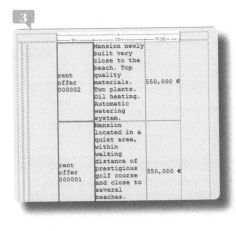

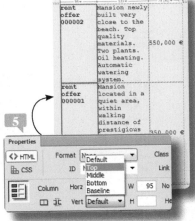

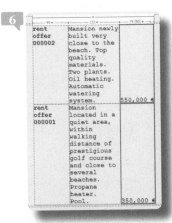

Importing and exporting tabular data

DREAMWEAVER LETS YOU EXPORT TABULAR DATA to a text file with the content of cells separated by a delimiter. When you export you generate a .csv data extension file that only exports the data contained in the cells, not the format options of the original table. You can import tabular data generated in Dreamweaver or any other application, which is saved in a delimited text format. Importing tabular data consists of selecting a given data file and the applied delimiter to separate the data, and assigning format options to the table resulting from the importation.

1. Select the nested table in the last cell of the main table, go to **File** and select **Export**.

2. Verify that you can export the template's data and the data from an entire table, but not part of it, and click **Table**.

3. The **Export Table** dialog box determines export settings. The **Delimiter** field specifies which delimiter character should be used to separate the cells in the exported file. **Line breaks** specifies the operating system used to open the exported file. Maintain the predetermined options and click **Export**.

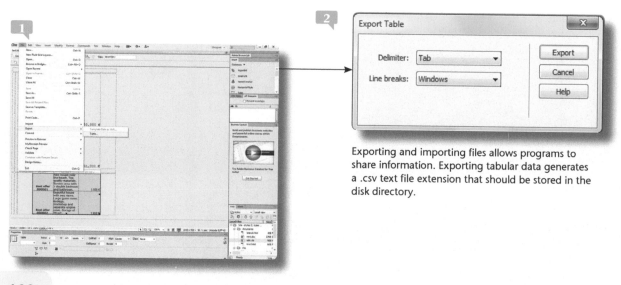

Exporting and importing files allows programs to share information. Exporting tabular data generates a .csv text file extension that should be stored in the disk directory.

045

4. The **Export Table AS** dialog box opens. Click the **File name** box and type the word **rent**. Click the **Desktop** button in the Direct Access panel.

5. After assigning a name and selecting the location, click **Save** to generate the text file.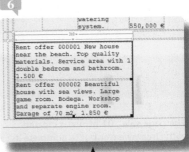

6. Delete the table so that you learn how to retrieve the data by importing it. Click **Delete**.

7. Open the **File** menu, click **Import** and select **Tabular Data**.

8. The **Import Tabular Data** dialog box opens. To import tabular data you must first select the file containing the information. Click **Browse** and click on the **Desktop** shortcut and double-click the **rent** file.

9. Once you have established the data source document, click the **Set to** option.

10. Click the field to the right and type the value **310**, click the arrow in **Percent** and select **Pixels**.

11. Double-click **Border**, press **Delete** and then click **OK** to permanently import data.

12. The program generates the table. The exported file preserves only the data, not the settings for table formatting, which is why the generated table only displays the attributes established in the Import dialog box. Close the page and click **Yes** in the warning menu to save the changes.

> ### IMPORTANT
>
> The table Import dialog box establishes the width of the generated table when importing it. The default setting option **Fit To Data** determines that the table width is defined by the imported tabular data itself.

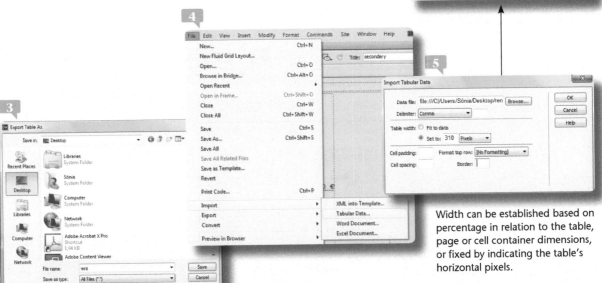

Width can be established based on percentage in relation to the table, page or cell container dimensions, or fixed by indicating the table's horizontal pixels.

Working with Expanded Tables Mode

DREAMWEAVER PROVIDES TWO TABLE MODES. The default mode is the Standard mode you already saw in previous exercises. But the program also has the Expanded Tables Mode. To switch go to the options in the Table Mode submenu in the View menu or use the buttons in the Design category in the Insert panel. It is recommended you return to the Standard mode when formatting the table.

1. Go to our download site and download and copy the **sale_01.htm** document and paste it in the **styles** site folder, and then locate it in the **Files** panel and double-click it to open.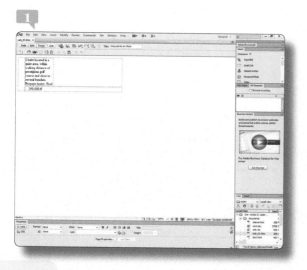

2. The page contains two nested tables in the last column of the main table. In the previous exercise you learned the Standard table insertion and editing mode. But Dreamweaver has another option available. Go to the **View** menu and click **Expanded Tables Mode** in the **Table Mode** submenu.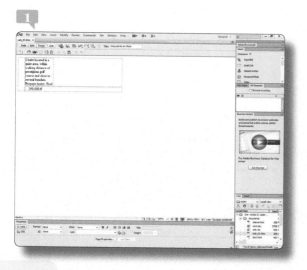

3. The Expanded Table Mode temporarily adds cell padding and spacing and increases the table's borders to make select-

The page **sale _01.htm** was created with Dreamweaver but to complete its content, tables generated in Microsoft Office applications were used.

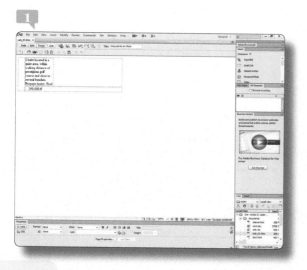

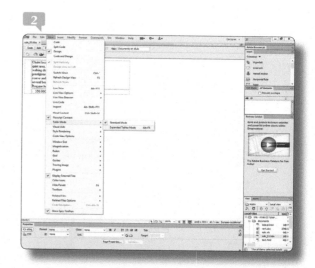

046

ing table elements easier. Look at the options in the **Getting Started in Expanded Table Mode** dialog box, enable the **Don't show me this message again** and press **OK**.

4. Click and place the edit cursor inside the first cell of the table and click **Image** in the **Insert** panel.

5. Next, insert one of the images you stored in the **styles** site **ima** folder, in an earlier exercise. Open the folder and double-click on the **gra_v01.jpg** file to insert the image.

6. To return to the Standard table mode you can use the options in the Menu Bar and, in this case, click the **exit** link that appears on the top of the window document.

7. The mode change can be made from the **Insert** panel. Select the **Layout** category in the **Insert** panel.

8. This category displays the buttons that activate the available table modes. Click the **Expanded** button in the **Insert** panel and switch back to the Standard mode by clicking that same button.

9. To finish, press the key combination **Ctrl + S** to save the changes.

You can also exit the Expanded Tables Mode by enabling the Standard mode in the **View** menu of the **Layout** tab in the **Insert** panel.

The **Expanded Tables Mode** facilitates the selection of the content of the cells or close to the cells.

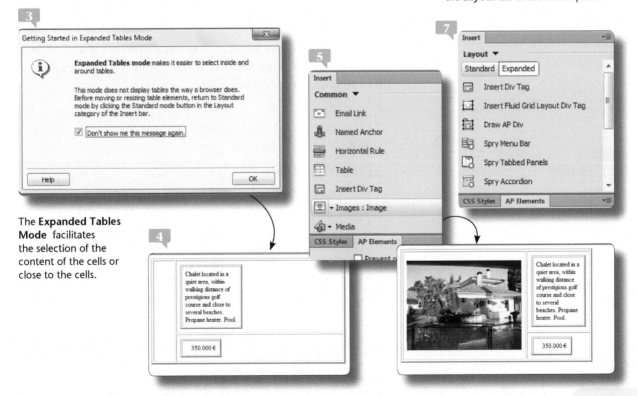

Working with CSS styles

BY DEFAULT, DREAMWEAVER applies Cascading Style Sheets (CSS) text formatting. The Preference dialog box includes the CSS styles category where Dreamweaver enters the code that determines styles. The use of CSS styles increases the settings possibilities for page properties. The Page Properties dialog box category defines links and headers, and the Appearance category provides complementary options.

1. Up until now you have used HTML tags instead of CSS styles to format the elements of a page. Open the **Edit** menu and select **Preferences**.

2. The use of styles adds great flexibility and control over the appearance of a page. **CSS styles** have a special category in the **Preferences** dialog box; enable it.

3. The CSS styles can write in an abbreviated style that is simpler and easier for users. But we recommend disregarding it since some browser versions don't interpret this form correctly. Press **OK**.

4. The use of CSS styles implies that Dreamweaver uses CSS tags for all the properties defined in the **Page Properties** dialog box categories. Click it now.

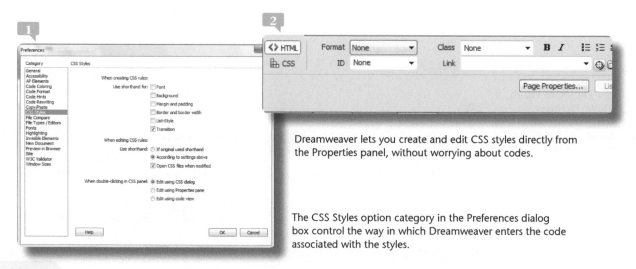

Dreamweaver lets you create and edit CSS styles directly from the Properties panel, without worrying about codes.

The CSS Styles option category in the Preferences dialog box control the way in which Dreamweaver enters the code associated with the styles.

047

5. The **Appearance (CSS)** category defines the predetermined font combination for the page. Open the **Page Font** category and select font combination **Verdana, Geneva, sans-serif**.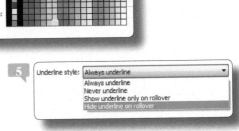

6. The use of CSS styles allows the application of bold and italic font and the selection of the size of the font for the text in a predetermined form. Press the arrow of the **Size** field and select the value **12**.

7. Click the **Background Color** dialog box and select light blue.

8. Select the **Links (CSS)** category.

9. In addition to the color of the hypertext according to its status, the category determines font, size, and predetermined attributes for hypertext or vary its underlining style. Open the display **Underline style** and select **Hide underline on rollover**.

10. Activate the **Headings (CSS)** category, press the arrow button of the **Header 2** field and select the option **18 pixels**.

11. Click the color dialog box that corresponds to the header that is being modified. Select blue intense and click **OK**.

12. Click the first cell in the table, while pressing **Ctrl**, and click **Insert Row Above** in the **Insert** panel and finish the exercise.

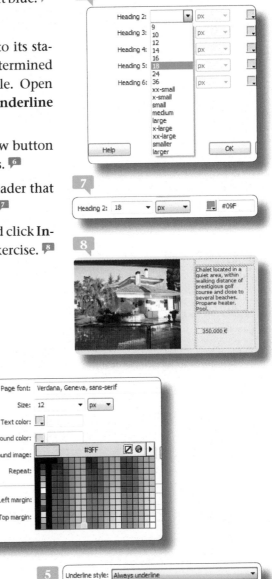

By default, size is referenced in pixels. The drop-down menu to the right of the Size filed determines the size reference used.

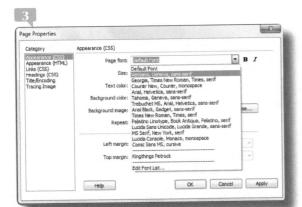

Applying CSS styles

CASCADE STYLE SHEETS (CSS) DETERMINE THE FORMAT and aspect of pages. CSS styles define many properties that cannot be accessed through HTML tags. To make it easier, Dreamweaver provides sample style sheets that can be applied to pages or used as starting points for more personalized styles. These will be explained later in this book.

1. Go to the **Files** panel, open the **Show** dialog box and select the **Elemental** site.

2. Locate and open the **index.htm** file.

3. The format previously applied to the first paragraph of the page, consisting of one word, is **Heading 1**. Double-click the first term of the page, **FriendHouse**, and click **Copy** in the **Standard** toolbar.

4. Note that the **h1** tag defining the properties of heading 1 is selected in the Status Bar. Click and activate the **sale_01 page.**

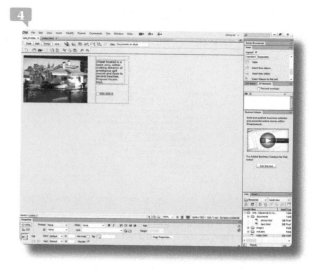

`<body> <h1>`

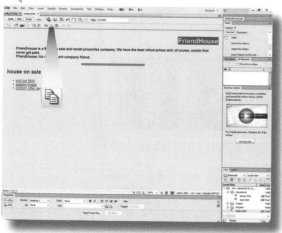

108

048

5. Click the bottom of the page, select **Paste** in the **Standard** toolbar and notice that the term loses the header format. [5]

6. Select the just pasted term and click **Cut** in the **Standard** toolbar. [6]

7. Click inside the first cell in the second column of the table and click **Paste**. [7]

8. The predetermined format for **Header 2** was defined in the **Page Properties** dialog box in the previous exercise. Click on the cell while pressing the **Ctrl** key.

9. A size of 18 pixels and the color blue was defined for this type of heading. Press the arrow button in the **Format** drop-down menu in the **Page Properties** dialog box and select the **Heading 2** option. [8]

10. Verify that the **Header 2** characteristics established in the category **(CSS) Headings** in the **Page Properties** dialog box are correctly applied to the selection. To finish this simple exercise, click the Close button of the current page and press **Yes** in the warning pop-up menu to save the changes.

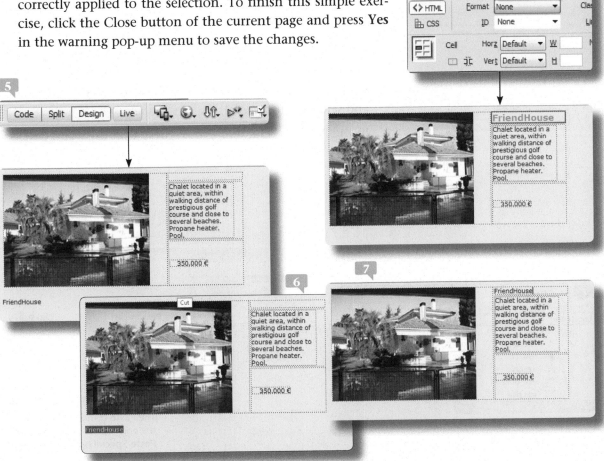

Applying demo style sheets

TO MAKE IT EASIER, Dreamweaver provides demo styles sheets that can be applied on pages or serve as starting points to define personalized styles. These are CSS style sheets that are stored as .css extension files. To attach these files to the pages, they must be stored in a current site folder. The program stores the demo style sheets in a CSS folder located in a higher level of the site. The CSS Styles panel facilitates access to the Attach External Style Sheet dialog box, linking with the sample style sheets provided by the program.

1. Add a new, blank, page with the name **top.htm** in the **styles** site's documents folder and open it. After completing this necessary step, open the **index.htm** page in the **Elemental** site and select the first two paragraphs.

2. Press **Copy** to copy the selected paragraphs and close the page.

3. The idea is to remove the original format of the copied text. With the opened **top.htm** document, go to the **Edit** menu and select **Paste Special**.

4. In the **Paste Special** dialog box, press **Text only** and **OK**.

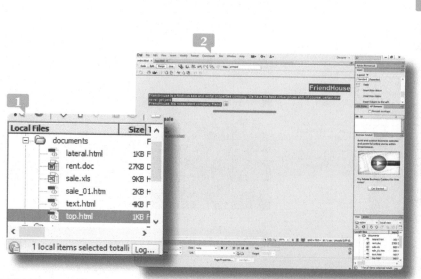

The **Paste** command maintains the original HTML format; use the **Paste Special** option in the Edit menu to remove it.

5. The text loses its original format, showing the page's normal predetermined text attributes. To define the page properties you will use an external style sheet. The first button in the lower right section of the **CSS Styles** panel, **Attach Style Sheet**, allows the use of CSS styles defined in external documents; click it.

6. The **Attach External Style Sheet** function allows you to select a set of styles stored in an external .css extension file. Click the **sample style sheets** link.

7. In the **Sample Style Sheets** dialog box click **Colors: Gray/Brown**. 6

8. For the page to be correctly attached to the selected style sheet, the style sheet should be stored in one of the site's folder. To permanently attach the selected sample style sheet, press **OK**.

9. The page has been correctly attached, although it cannot be visualized in the style panel on the right. Press the **All** button in the **CSS Styles** panel to show the new style sheet.

10. Once you've attached the style sheet, which appears with the name **colors3.css** 7 in the **CSS Styles** panel, the format rules in it are applied to the page. To finish the exercise click **Save** in the **Standard** toolbar.

The **CSS Styles** panel lets you create, edit, and remove CSS styles. In the current page, because no style is being used, it has no content.

The CSS file can be attached to a page or embedded in the page's header.

Defining HTML style tags

CSS STYLE SHEETS CONTAIN three kinds of format rules: style-defining tags, class styles, and identification styles. The HTML style tags redefine the format of a given tag, affecting all the page elements attached to the said tag. Regardless of which type, a CSS style rule consists of two parts: the selector and the declaration. The selector identifies the style or tag, and the declaration defines the elements that form the style. The declaration also consists of two parts: the defined property and the assigned value.

1. Go to the **Files** panel, click the boxed + preceding the **styles** site's **CSS** folder and verify that the **colors3.css** styles sheet is correctly stored in it.

2. View how the file is attached to the page. Press the **Code** button in the Document toolbar.

3. The sample style sheet file, **colors3.css**, is automatically attached to the page through a reference located in the page's header, the **head** section of the document. 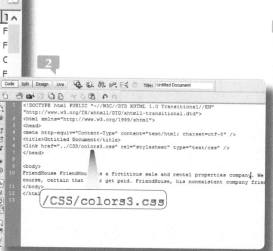 Return to **Design** view.

4. You can edit the style sheets directly in Dreamweaver. Double-click the **colors3.css** document in the **Files** panel.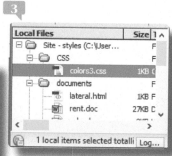

5. The first rule of this style sheet defines the page background color. The selector is the tag corresponding to the **body** and

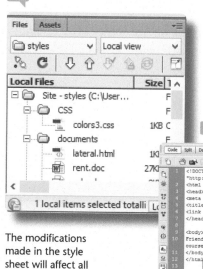

The modifications made in the style sheet will affect all the pages attached to it.

The HTML tag corresponding to the attached style sheet is <link href>.

the declaration consists of the background color property and its heximal value. The selectors can be multiple as in the case of the second rule, which means that the definition affects several tags. Double-click the Hex value, **666633**, corresponding to the property defined in the second rule.

6. This rule controls the colors of the text of several tags, the text of the page, body, and headers. Write the value, **00000**, 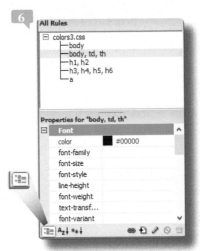 corresponding to the color black, click the Close button in the **colors3.css** page and click **Yes** in the warning pop-up menu to save the changes made.

7. The color black defined in the style sheet is automatically applied to the page's text.  In the CSS Styles panel select the second rule defined in the **colors3.css** style sheet and click **Show Category View**, the first button in the bottom left section of the **Properties** subpanel.

8. Double-click the property **font-family**, click the arrow button displayed and choose, **Arial, Helvetica, sans-serif**.

9. Double-click on the **colors3.css** style in the CSS Styles panel to view the code in the window.

10. Double-click the **h2** expression of the tenth code line and click **Delete** so the text with the Header 2 format don't contain variations when the style rule is applied. Click the **Back** key twice to eliminate the extra comma and space and click **Ctrl + S** to save the changes made to the code in the style sheet and finish the exercise.

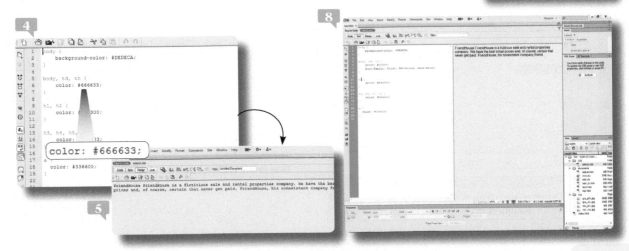

Working with related files

DREAMWEAVER EFFICIENTLY MANAGES web files thanks to the Related Files function. This function activates the program's Split view, showing the source code of the related files in Code view and, the main page, in Design view.

1. When a sample style sheet is applied the **Related Files** toolbar, displaying the name of the sheet, appears in the Dreamweaver workspace. As shown in the previous exercise, the **Split** view now displays the code of the related file and design of your web page. To show this source code, click the **Source Code** button.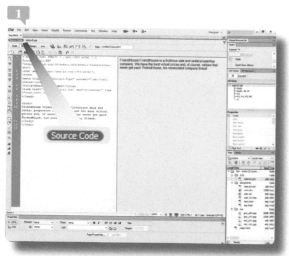

2. The corresponding page code being edited appears in the **Code** view. To show the style sheet code again, click the style sheet, click on its name, **colors3.css**, in the **Related Files** toolbar.

3. To open the related file from the toolbar, right-click the file name and select the only option appearing in the context menu, **Open as Separate File**.

The order of the toolbar buttons follows the order of the links in the existing related files.

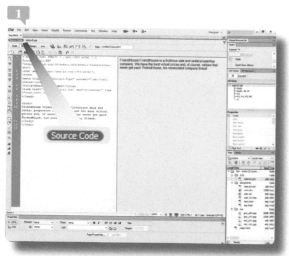

By default, Dreamweaver displays the names of all files related to a main document in the Related Files toolbar.

051

4. Logically, when the related file is opened, the main page assumes a secondary level. Close the **colors3.css** file. [3]

5. Related files are visualized in different ways. Open the **View** menu and disable **Split Vertically.**

6. The main page's design is shown in the upper part of the document window and the related file above the Design View of the document. Open the **View** menu again and click **Design View on Top.** [4]

7. The related file and main page are shown in reversed position. Select **Design View on Left** in the **View** menu to return to the original view modes.

8. Learn to disable related files so that they don't appear in the document's window. Open the **Edit** menu and click **Preferences**.

9. Select the **General** category and notice that the **Enable Related Files** option is selected. [5] Maintain the selection as is and close the Preferences dialog box to finish the exercise. Click **Cancel.**

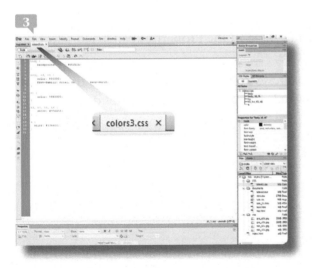

By default, when you open a related file in Design or Split view, the related file is displayed above the Design view of the document.

If a related file is missing, Dreamweaver still displays the corresponding button, but when you click the button nothing appears on the screen.

6

Document options: ☑ Show Welcome Screen
☑ Reopen documents on startup
☑ Warn when opening read-only files
☑ Enable Related Files

Editing style sheets

IMPORTANT

The **Edit Styles Sheet** function in the CSS Styles panel varies according to the function of the selected element in the panel. If the selected element is a rule, the rule assistant appears to modify it, and, if it is a style sheet, the corresponding code appears, in the Design View.

YOU CAN EDIT STYLE SHEETS directly in Dreamweaver by adding the corresponding rule code or using the options in the Properties panel to modify the predetermined properties; although this is not recommended for beginners. To simplify this task the program provides a styles rule definition assistant. The assistant organizes the properties in different categories, the first of which, Type, provides options related to text formatting.

1. Start by separating the Title Header from the rest of the paragraph by clicking **Enter**. Next, select the first term of the page, **FriendHouse**.

2. The style sheet applied, **colors3.css**, uses the second rule to control the format of normal text on the page. Therefore, the selected paragraph controlled by the **body** tag, appears in black and the font combination **Arial, Helvetica, sans-serif**. The next rule, with several selectors or tags, controls the format of the different types of headers. Click the arrow button of the **Format** field in the **Properties** panel and select the **Heading 2** option.

3. In a previous exercise the selector that controlled this type of header was deleted. Therefore, its format is not dependent on

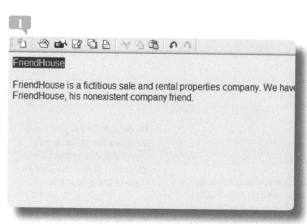

When a rule is modified, the style sheet containing it is opened and changed.

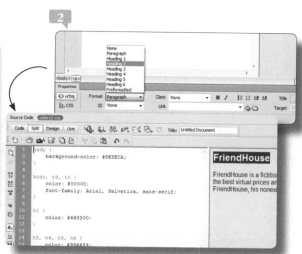

116

the CSS style sheet but on the HTML tags. Instead, the style sheet does control the format of other types of headers, such as Header 4, corresponding to tag h4, in the third rule. Select the first term of the second paragraph, click the **Format** button and select the option **Heading 4.**

4. The paragraph automatically adopts the established format, and the style rule that controls this tag is applied. In the **CSS Styles** panel select the rule applied to **h3, h4, h5,** and **h6** and press the **Edit rule** icon, represented by a pencil image.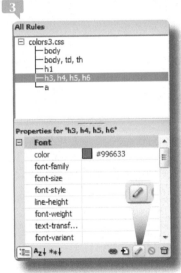

5. The **Type** category allows the text properties to be altered. The selected rule controls only the color of the text having the h3, h4, h5, and h6 header format. Click the arrow in the Color field and select a color sample. Verify the change is made by clicking **OK.**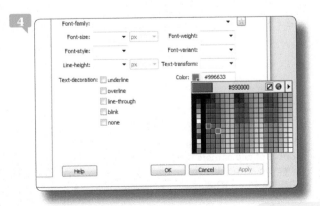

6. The external style sheet is modified at the same time the rule's new value is applied to the paragraph of the page having the Heading 4 format. Double-click the same rule you just edited in the **CSS Styles** panel.

7. In this way, the program manages the selected rule's definition assistant. Press **OK.**

8. Click on the name of the style sheet **colors3.css** and press the **Edit Styles Sheet.**

9. The style sheet code is displayed in Code View in the document window. 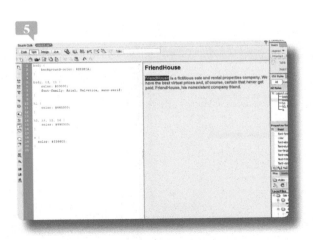 Press the **Design** button on the Document toolbar and open the File menu and select **Save All.**

Remember that to apply a style to a paragraph you do not have to select the entire paragraph.

Creating new style rules

CREATING NEW STYLE RULES IS EASY, all you need to do is select the sheet in the CSS Styles panel and start to edit. Click the New CSS Rule button in the CSS Styles panel and enter the selector name in the window you will see with the same name. There are three types of rules: tag defining, class and identification, or advanced. Once the name has been selected, the program takes you to the style definition assistant that, sorted by categories, lets you make a visual selection of the corresponding value for each modifiable property.

1. To start, select the style sheet, **colors3.css**, in the **CSS Styles** panel and, in the Properties pane, click the **New CSS Rule** button showing a document with a + to the left.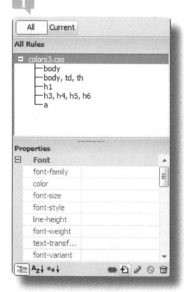

2. So far you have practiced with defining tag styles, but there is also class and identifier or advanced styles. The **New CSS Rule** dialog box, by default, creates predetermined class styles. Click the **Selector Type** button and click the **Tag** option.

3. Enter the tag reference that will be defined by the style rule, meaning the selector, in the next field. Click the arrow button of the **Selector Name** drop-down menu, scroll down until you find the **h3** tag and select it.

The style rules redefine the format of one or more tags, affecting all the elements using that tag on the page.

In the New CSS Rule dialog box, select the type of rule that you will create in the Selector Type menu.

053

4. Select the option by which the rule will be defined in the **colors3.css** style sheet, and click **OK**.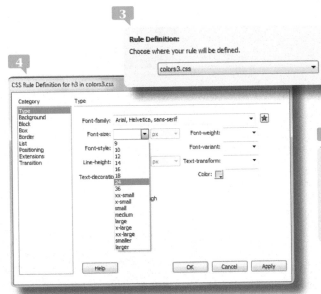

5. The style defining assistant, with the configurable properties, automatically pops up. Click the arrow button in the **Font-family** field and select font combination, **Arial, Helvetica, sans-serif**.

6. Click the arrow button of the **Font-size** field box and select the value **24**.

7. Assign a color to the defined text using the new style tag. Click the arrow point in the **Color** field, select your favorite color and, once the properties of the new rule have been defined, click **OK**.

8. Next, apply the **Heading 3** format to the page title and watch how it adjusts the configured properties for the new style rule controlling this type of tag.

9. Click the **Page Properties** button in the **Properties** panel.

10. Click the **Headings (CSS)** category in the **Page Properties** dialog box and, once verified that the page properties corresponding to the text with the **Heading 3** format have been modified, click **OK**.

11. To finish, save the changes made, both in the **top.htm** page as in the **colors3.css styles sheet.** Open the **File** menu and select **Save All**.

A rule can be defined in the style sheet only for an active document or new style sheet that will later be attached to your page.

FriendHouse

FriendHouse is a fictitious sale and rental prices and, of course, certain that never ge friend.

When you edit an external style sheet, all the attached documents are affected.

Attaching external style sheets

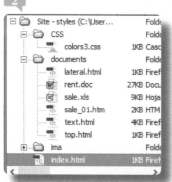
EXTERNAL STYLE SHEETS can be attached to a page either by importing them, which means the inclusion of a style tag in the header of the page, or by a link, which means the inclusion in the page header of an **href** tag link containing the URL of the external style sheet.

1. Select the term **FriendHouse** in the second line of the page and click **Copy**.

2. The copied paragraph has the **Heading 3** format. Copy it to the **index.htm** page of the **styles** site, created in earlier exercises where the properties were defined using HTML tags. In the **Files** panel, locate the mentioned file, 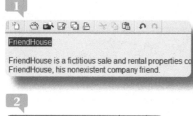 double-click it to open and click **Paste** in the Standard toolbar.

3. The paragraph loses the original page properties because they were linked to the style sheet attached to the **colors3.css** page. The background color was defined with HTML tags. Activate the **Code** View.

4. In this case, the only property specified is the background color for the **body** tag, the code of which is displayed in line 8.  Return to **Design** View and, in the **CSS Styles** panel, click the **Attach Style Sheets** button.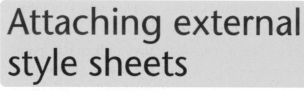

FriendHouse

FriendHouse is a fictitious sale and rental properties c...
FriendHouse, his nonexistent company friend.

In previous Dreamweaver versions, the selection of the use of CSS Styles in the preferences automatically generated the necessary code to embed the style that defined the page's properties.

5. The **Attach External Style Sheet** dialog box opens. The **File/URL** field box recognizes the location of the external style sheet used at an earlier time. Enable **Import**.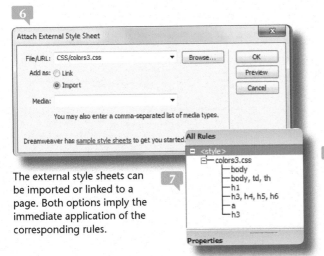

6. The main difference between attaching and importing external styles is in how conflicting properties are resolved when rules overlap in external style sheets that are linked as opposed to imported into a page. Click **OK**.

7. Now, the **CSS Styles** panel reflects the use of an embedded style. Click the + preceding the **colors3.css** page.

8. The imported style sheet is dependent of a style embedded in the header of the page. Click the **Format** button in the **Properties** panel and select **Heading 3**.

9. Click the **Code** button and verify that the **style** tag in the page's header recognizes the import reference of the external style sheet.

10. Return to **Design** view, select the **colors3.css** style sheet in the **CSS Styles** panel and click the **Unlink CSS style sheet** icon, represented by the image of a trash can.

11. Notice how the paragraph shows the Heading 3 format but without the style defined in the sheet. Click **Attach Style Sheet** in the panel while pressing the **Link** option and click **OK**.

12. The **CSS Styles** panel displays the linked, but independent, style sheet. Activate **Code** view, and after verifying that the link is correctly recognized in the **href** tag, on line 8 of the code concerning the URL where the external style sheet is located, return to **Design** view and **Save**.

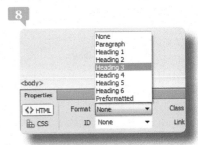

The external style sheets can be imported or linked to a page. Both options imply the immediate application of the corresponding rules.

121

Generating CSS-based documents

WHEN YOU CREATE A NEW PAGE IN DREAMWEAVER, you can create one containing a predetermined CSS design. Dreamweaver has over 16 different CSS designs for you to choose from. Or, you can also create your own CSS designs and add them to the configuration folder so that they appear in the list of available designs in the New Document dialog box.

1. Go to the **File** menu and select **New**.

2. The first step is to select the type of page you wish to create in the **New Document** dialog box. For this exercise, select the Blank Page option and click **HTML** page type.

3. There are 16 predetermined CSS designs in the Design category to choose from. The 16 designs are divided among those containing fixed tables and those containing liquid tables. Fixed tables have fixed column dimensions specified in pixels that do not change because of the size or configuration of browsers. The width of the liquid tables is defined as a percentage of the visitor's browser width. Click on the **2 column fixed, right sidebar**.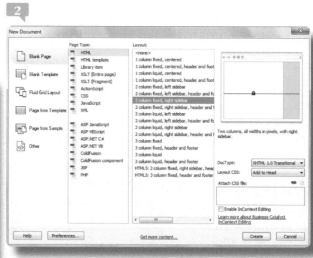

4. You can see the appearance of the selected design in the sidebar previewing space provided. Maintain the predetermined selected option, **XHTML 1.0 Transitional**, in the **Type of Document** field. In the **Layout CSS** you can select either, **Add to Head**, **Create New File**, or **Link to Existing File**. With this last option you can specify a CSS file containing predetermined design rules. Because you already have a CSS file, select this third option. ▣

5. To select the necessary file, click **Attach Style Sheet**, in the **Attach CSS file** field. ▣

6. The **Attach External Style Sheet** dialog box opens. Look to see if the **colors3.css** document appears in the **File/URL** field. (If you can't see it, locate it in the **CSS** folder in the **styles** site.) Click **OK**. ▣

7. When a page is linked to a CSS file, the CSS design selected in the dialog box will adjust to the linked file. Click **Create** to create the new document with the starter CSS design. ▣

8. See the design of the new page and note that users' instructions are included. To finish, click the Close button to exit the page.

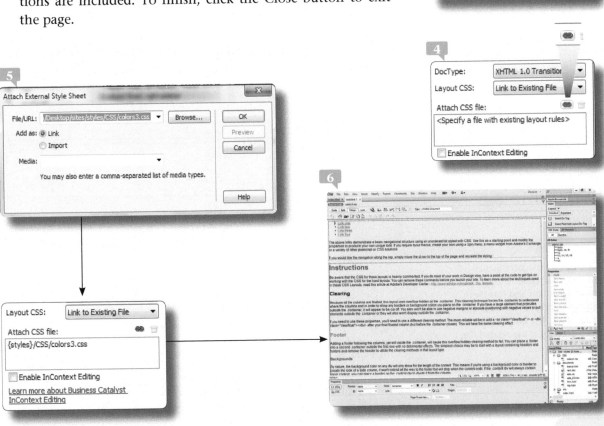

Showing a selection code

DREAMWEAVER HAS A CODE BROWSER FUNCTION that shows all the code sources that affect a page selection at a given time. When clicking a link in the browser, Dreamweaver opens the file containing the corresponding code.

1. In this exercise you will learn how to work with the code navigator related to the CSS rules of the style sheet linked to the **index.htm** page of the **styles** site. You can access the code navigator from **Design, Code,** and **Split** view. Just press and hold the Alt key, while you click anywhere in the page or click on the **Code Navigator Indicator** that appears near the insertion point by default, when the mouse has been idle for more than 2 seconds. Click at the end of the term **FriendHouse**, while keeping the **Alt** key pressed.

2. The navigator code appears displaying the rules of the linked styles sheet, **colors3.css.** Before accessing one of the rules, click the verification box of the **Disable Indicator** option so that the indicator does not appear on the screen. You can re-enable the indicator anytime by going to the Code Navigator.

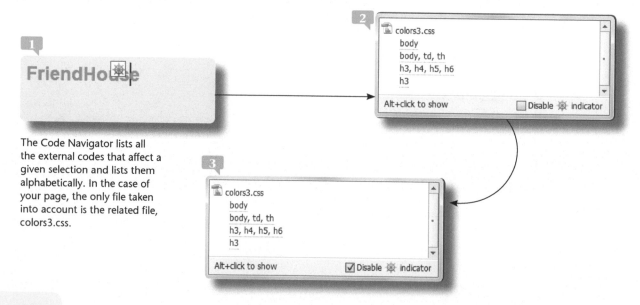

The Code Navigator lists all the external codes that affect a given selection and lists them alphabetically. In the case of your page, the only file taken into account is the related file, colors3.css.

056

3. Note that you can also access the Code Navigator by selecting that option in the **View** menu 🔲 or by clicking key combination **Ctrl + Alt + N**. Hover with the mouse pointer over the rule corresponding to the **h3** tag and, after verifying that an informative dialog box with the rule's properties appears on the screen, 🔲 click it.

4. Because it concerns a defined rule that is in the related file, **colors3.css**, the style sheet, the program displays the rule in **Split** view with the insertion point in the corresponding code line. 🔲 Return to **Design** view and click on the page again, while holding the **Alt** key.

5. The Code Navigator groups related code sources by file and lists the files alphabetically. Place the mouse pointer over the second rule, where the **body** and **td, th** tag properties are defined to see their properties in the Code view of the related file. 🔲

6. Click the **Source Code** button in the related Files toolbar to view the page code and not the code of the related file, **colors3.css**. 🔲

7. Note that you can also find the **Code Navigator Indicator** in the toolbar to the left of the code. 🔲 Click on the said icon to show again the navigator and, to finish this simple exercise, click the **Escape** key to hide it and return to **Design** View.

The descriptions of the rules appearing when you hover over them in the **Code Navigator** facilitates their identification, although some names are repeated.

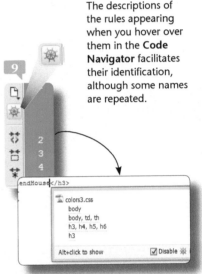

The Code Navigator indicator is not operative in the style sheet code.

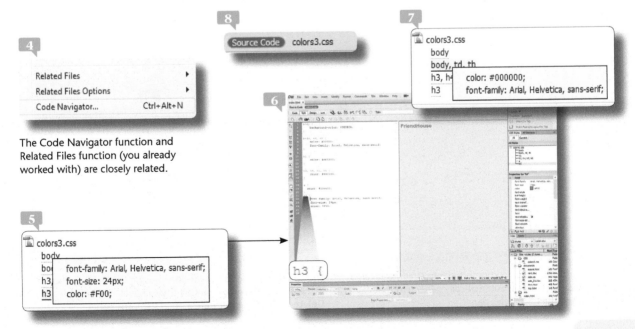

The Code Navigator function and Related Files function (you already worked with) are closely related.

125

Creating class styles

IMPORTANT

The reference to the element to which the class rule is applied appears in the first line of the element's code. In this case, **type**.

`<style type='`

CLASS STYLES can be applied to any element in the document, regardless of the tags that control them. You can always identify class styles or rules because their names are always preceded by a dot and they are stored in a style sheet, either external or internal. The header contains the reference to the style sheet while the page element, to which the class rule will be applied to, contains a reference to the class used in the tag corresponding to the page's body tag.

1. Open the **sale_01.htm** and **text.htm** pages in the **styles** site in Dreamweaver bringing the second **text.htm** document up front. All the style rules associated with the page that resulted from importing the Excel data are displayed in the **CSS Styles** panel, where there is also a list of the available class rules. Right-click the first style rule in the panel and, in the context menu, select **Delete**.

2. With the second style rule selected in the **CSS Styles** panel, click **Delete CSS Rule**.

3. Click **New CSS Rule**, the second button in the group located in the lower part of the **CSS Styles** panel.

When Word or Excel data is imported into Dreamweaver, a defined class style rule is automatically generated that can be viewed in the **CSS Styles** panel.

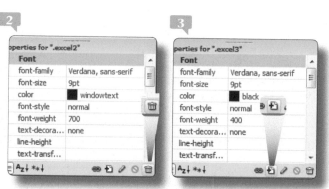

You can delete rules and style sheets using the Delete option in the context menu of the **CSS Styles** panel, or use the **Delete Styles Sheet** or **Rule** icon in the same panel.

057

4. Click the already selected **Class** option in the **Selector Type** field; enter the term **.type** in the name field box; 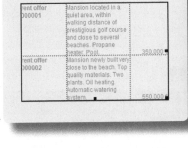 in the **Rule Definition** field select **New Style Sheet File** and click **OK**.

5. In the **Save Style Sheet File As** dialog box select the location for the **.css** file and name it. Select the **CSS** folder, click the **Name** field box and type the word **personal** and **Save**.

6. Modify a series of known properties. Select the font combination **Arial, Helvetica, sans-serif;** specify a size of **12 pixels**, and apply the color orange to the text and click **OK**.

7. The style sheet created, **personal.css**, is linked to the **text.htm** page. The sheet now has a defined class rule, although it hasn't been applied to any element on the page. This is because class styles, as opposed to defining tag styles, are applied on selected elements, regardless of the tag controlling them. Select the nested table in the upper part of the main table, display the **Class** field menu in the **Properties** panel and select **type** for the new class just created.

8. Apply this new class to the second nested table using the same procedure.

At the same time that the new class style sheet appears in the **CSS Styles** panel, the **Related Files** toolbar is activated displaying the name assigned to the sheet.

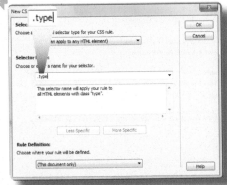

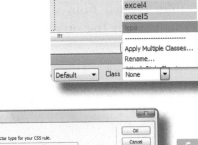

A style rule has to be either embedded or linked to an attached **external sheet**.

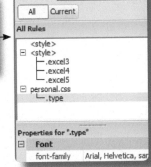

A dot preceding the name distinguishes the class styles. If you forget, the program inserts the dot automatically.

Duplicating class styles

IMPORTANT

The **Duplicate** option that opens the **Duplicate CSS Rule** dialog box is located in the CSS Styles panel.

DUPLICATE STYLE RULES facilitate the creation of new rules based on the original properties. During the creation process you can assign the new rule, the duplicate, to the sheet containing the original rule, to another sheet used in the site, or to a new style sheet. The duplicate can be modified later from the style definition assistant by creating a variation of the original rule. Style sheets are duplicated from the Edit Style Sheet menu.

1. The **personal.css** style sheet has one rule called **type**. Go to the **CSS Styles** panel and click the boxed + next to the sheet, right-click on the rule and, in the context menu, click **Duplicate**.

2. In the **Duplicate CSS Rule** dialog box assign a name to the new class rule. Click **Selector Name** and enter the term **.type_n** and click **OK**.

3. The duplicate is stored in the same style sheet, the **personal.css** sheet, as the original rule. In the **CSS Styles** panel double-click the new rule, the duplicated one, to edit.

4. Contrary to the rules created from scratch, the new rule has set properties defined in the original rule. Display the

Unless otherwise indicated, the duplicated rule is stored in the same sheet as the original.

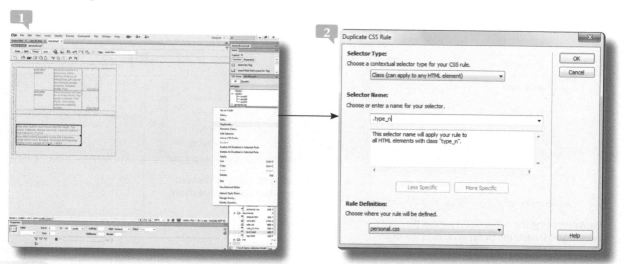

058

Font-weight menu and select the **bold** option to highlight the thickness of the font and click **OK**.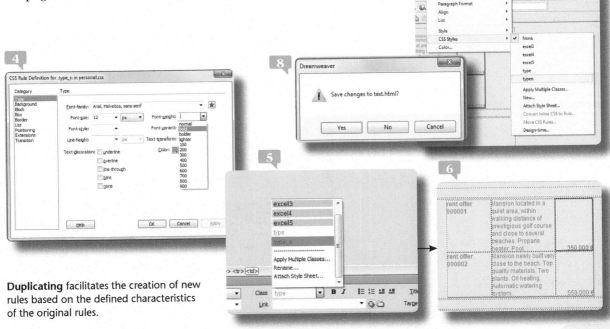

5. Click the cell containing the text **350.000€** while at the same time pressing the **Ctrl** key and click the arrow button in the **Class** field in the **Properties** panel.

6. In the inferior part of the menu there are the following command buttons: **Apply Multiple Classes** (a new feature in this version) to apply more than one class to the same element; **Attach Styles Sheet** that opens the **Attach External Style Sheet**, and **Change Name** that opens the **Change Style Name** dialog box. In the upper part there is a list of the applicable style rules. Select the **type_n** option.

7. The text included in the cell acquires the characteristics defined in the class rule. Press key combination **Ctrl + Z** to undo the last modification made.

8. Now apply the new rule to the third column of the first embedded table following a different procedure. Select the column, open the **Format** menu and click **CSS Styles**.

9. Notice the submenu also lists the created styles. Select the **type_n** option.

10. To finish, close the **text.htm** page and click **Yes** in the dialog boxes asking if you want to save the changes made on the page and on the linked style sheet.

IMPORTANT

The **None** command in the **Class** field of the Properties panel removes the application of a class style for a selected element.

excel3
excel4
excel5

In addition to the options available in the **Class** section of the Properties panel, the CSS Styles submenu of the Format menu provides more alternatives.

Duplicating facilitates the creation of new rules based on the defined characteristics of the original rules.

129

Applying multiple CSS classes

WITH DREAMWEAVER YOU CAN APPLY MULTIPLE CSS CLASSES to a single element. The program has a Multiclass Selection dialog box from where you choose the classes you wish to apply. After applying the multiple classes, the program creates a new multiclass that will be available in other locations where CSS selections are being made.

1. To begin, retrieve the **text.htm** page in the **styles** site used in the previous exercise to create a duplicate of an existing style rule. Practice applying several multiple rules to a single element on the page. Select the text **rent ofer 000001** in the second nested table.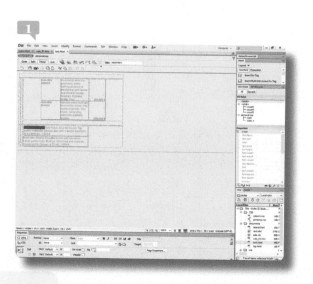

2. Dreamweaver provides several access points to the **Multiclass Selection** dialog box, from the CSS Properties panel **Targeted Rule**, from the **Class** menu in the **HTML** section also in the Properties panel, or from the context menu of the tag corresponding to the selected element. In this case follow the first procedure: go to the **CSS** section in the **Properties** panel, display the **Targeted Rule** box and click **Apply Multiple classes.**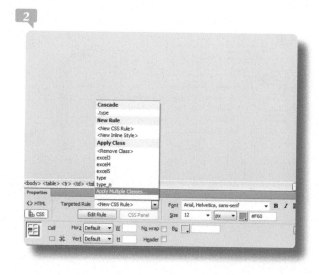

3. The **Multiclass Selection** dialog box opens showing the list of available classes for the current document. Verify that, in this case, the selected class **type** is applied to the chosen element. 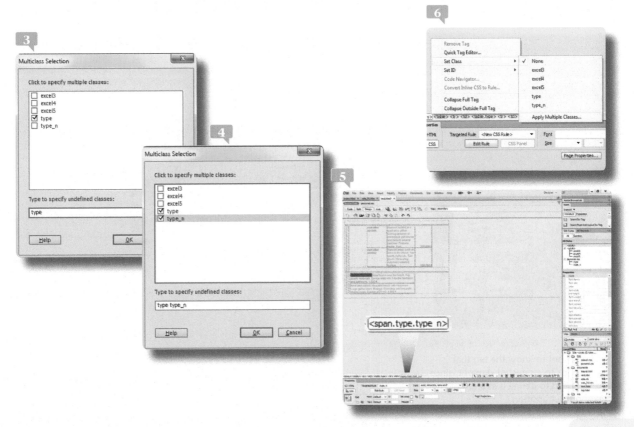 Check the verification box of the **type_n** class to select it.

4. The selected classes are gradually added to the field below, or you can also enter them manually by typing the names of the undefined classes separated by one space. Click **OK** to apply the two classes on the selected element.

5. With the text element still selected, pay attention to the corresponding tag in the tag selector. The name of the two applied classes is reflected. Select the **<body>** tag in the tag selector.

6. Next, right-click the tag, go to **Set Class** and, after verifying that you can also apply individual classes from this same submenu, select **Apply Multiple Classes**.

7. As mentioned, this is another form of accessing the **Multiclass Selection** dialog box. Exit the dialog box by clicking **OK** and close the current page without saving the changes made.

Working with the new CSS Transitions panel

IMPORTANT

You can create an external style sheet based on the CSS3 transition. For this, select **New Styles Sheet File** in the field **Choose Where to Create the Transition** of the New Transition dialog box. Select an external sheet based on the CSS transition. When the transition creation process is finished you will be prompted to specify a location to store the new CSS file.

A NEW FEATURE OF THE CS6 VERSION IS THE USE of CSS Transition panels to apply smooth changes in properties of page elements according to action or event applied: hover, click, or focus. You can select these transitions from the new CSS Transition panel.

1. In this exercise you will practice creating a transition based on CSS styles on the **sale_01.htm** page currently opened in the Dreamweaver workspace. The specific objective is to create an effect that will increase the size of the title **FriendHouse** when hovering with the mouse pointer. While pressing the **Ctrl** key, click the cell containing the mentioned title.

2. Go to the New Transition panel. Display the **Window** menu and click on the command **CSS Transitions**.

3. The panel is simple and for the moment empty. Press the boxed + to initiate the transition creation process.

4. The **New Transition** dialog box opens to create the transition class. The **Target Rule** field is where you specify the transition

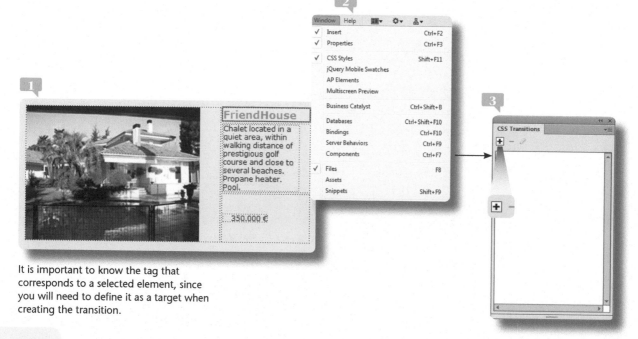

It is important to know the tag that corresponds to a selected element, since you will need to define it as a target when creating the transition.

060

selector name. The selector can be a tag, an ID, or a compound selector. In this case, display the field and select the **h2** tag.

5. In the **Transition On** field specify the type of event that will trigger the transition, in this case select **hover**.

6. In the **Duration** field, insert the value 2 press it for a while and, in this case, leave the **Delay** field blank, so that the transition is immediate.

7. The timing function refers to the transition style applied. Display the field and select **ease**.

8. This field indicates the property that will be carried out with the transition. Click the + next to the bottom of this field and select **font-size** from the long list of properties.

9. Verify that the **End-Value** field is activated. The content in this field varies according to the selected property. In this case, insert the value **35** as the size for the end of the transition and click **Create Transition**.

10. The details of the transition appear on the panel. The last step is to verify the end result. To do this save the changes made, look at it in your browser, hover over the title, **Friend-House**, and notice how the size increases correctly.

IMPORTANT

Once the CSS transitions are created, they can be edited from the CSS Transition panel. Select the transition and click the Edit selected transition icon, represented by the image of a pencil. To delete, click the icon with the – sign.

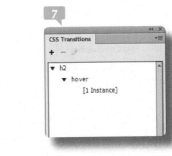

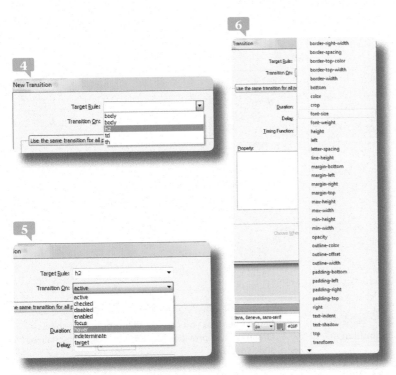

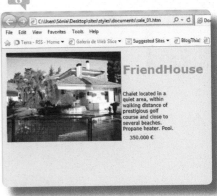

Delay is the time, in seconds or milliseconds, before the transition starts.

Combining style sheets

CSS STYLE PAGE PROPERTIES implies the creation of style sheets embedded with tag rules. Pages can be linked to more than one external style sheet. Note that while using pages containing tag rules can lead to conflicts, combining style sheets containing tag rules with style sheets containing class rules is recommended.

1. Open the **sale_01.htm** file, open the **CSS Styles** panel and select the embedded style.

2. Since the **colors3.css** style sheet tag rules are similar to the properties defined in the **sale_01.htm** page, click **Delete Embedded Stylesheet**.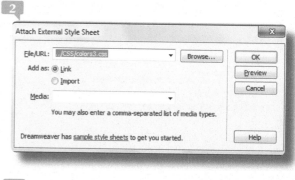

3. Click the **Attach Style Sheet** command in the **CSS Styles** panel.

4. Select the **colors3** page and click **OK**. 2

5. Click **Attach Style Sheet** again and press the **Browse** option in the **Attach External Style Sheet** dialog box.

6. Double-click the **personal.css** file, to permanently attach the style sheet, and click **OK**. 3

Verify that the last class style responds to the CSS transition created in the previous exercise.

Remember that you can use the sample style sheets Dreamweaver provides as a base for your personalized style sheets.

061

7. The elements controlled by the tag rules defined in the **colors3.css** style sheet show the established properties. With the **personal.css** page selected in the panel, click **New CSS Rule**.

8. The new rule will be included in the **personal.css** style sheet containing class rules only. Type **.tables** in the **Selector Name** field box; select the **personal.css** style sheet in the **Rule Definition** field and click **OK**.

9. Go to the **Background** category, click the arrow in **Background-color** and select a violet color tone from the color chart.

10. Go to the **Border** category that determines the settings of the borders surrounding the elements. Click the arrow in the **Top** field box of the **Style** section and select **solid**.

11. In the **Width** section, select **thick**.

12. Select a dark green tone for the borders and click **OK**.

13. Apply the new style rule to the main table of the page. Select the table, click the arrow in the **Class** field of the Properties panel and click the **tables** option.

14. Click outside the table to deselect it.

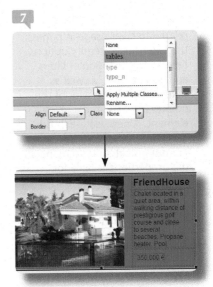

The appearance of the solid border style can change with some browsers, although the main browsers will maintain the settings established. Dreamweaver displays all solid styles in the document window.

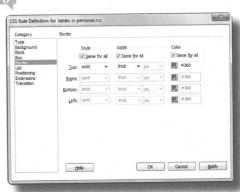

By default, the Same for All option is enabled in the three sections, which means that the properties assigned to the top border are also applied to the rest.

Defining categories for style rules

PROPERTY OPTIONS TO DEFINE STYLE RULES are listed by categories. The Block category determines settings for spacing and alignment. The Box category defines settings for tags and properties controlling page element placement. The List category defines size and type of bullets for lists that can be personalized by using image files specified for that purpose. The Extensions category contains options related to the inclusion of filters and page break options.

1. Select the cell containing the house description.

2. Include a new rule in the external sheet containing the class styles previously used. Duplicate one of the existing rules so that you don't have to begin from scratch. Go to the **CSS Styles** panel and, on the **personal.css** sheet, right-click the **type** class rule and select **Duplicate**.

3. Assign an ID name to the duplicate. Enter the term **.info** in the **Selector Name** field box and click **OK**.

4. To modify the **.info** class rule select it from the **CSS Styles** panel and click **Edit Rule**.

5. Access the **Background** category, located to the left side of the dialog box.

Don't forget: to be considered a class rule, the selector name always begins with a dot.

You can access the edit menu of a rule from either the context menu or from the CSS style panel's Option menu.

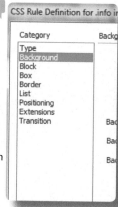

062

6. Click the arrow in **Background-color,** choose a light yellow tone from the color chart  and then go to the **Block** category.

7. Go to **Word Spacing** and substitute the existing text in the value option for the value **3** and, in the field box located on the right, select **px.**

8. Select **Right** in the **Text Align** field and activate the **Box** category.

9. The **Float** and **Clear** options are applicable only to pages containing layers. **Padding** determines the space between the content and its border or margin. **Margin** specifies the space allowed between a given element and the surrounding elements. Activate the **Border** category.

10. Open the **Top** dialog box in the **Style** section and select **solid.**

11. Click **Top** in the **Width** filed box and enter the value **1,** if you wish choose a border color and click **OK.**

12. Open the **Class** section in the **Properties** panel and select **info.** See the result.

13. Click **Save All** to store the changes made both in the **sale_01.htm** page and in the **personal.css** styles page.

The edited class rules are listed in the Class section in the Properties panel and are also available in the CSS Styles option of the Format menu.

Background-color:
Background-image: #FFC
Background-repeat:
Background-attachment:
Background-position (X):
Background-position (Y):

Style   Width
☑ Same for all   ☑ Same for all
Top: solid   1   px
Right: solid   1   px
Bottom: solid   1   px
Left: solid   1   px

None
info
tables
type
type_n

Apply Multiple Classes...
Rename...

Class x|24
Link

133 No wrap ☐ Bg ☐
Header ☐

Word-spacing: 3   px
Letter-spacing: em
Vertical-align: %
Text-align: right
Text-indent:
White-space:

The Letter Spacing field in the Block category determines additional space between value characters, increasing space with positive values, decreasing with negative values.

Creating ID style rules

IMPORTANT

With the **Compound** selector type you can create a rule or identifiers affecting two or more tags at the same time.

IN CONTRAST TO TAG AND CLASS DEFINITION RULES, advanced style rules are applied to elements containing a specific ID. Not all web page elements can be identified. When an element can be identified, a specific field in the Properties panel appears. Advanced style rules are identified by a pound sign preceding the name, and they can be stored in an external style sheet or simply embedded on the page header.

1. Apply an advanced style rule to the nested table containing the price of the house. Select the nested table in question and click **New CSS Rule** in the **CSS Styles** panel.

2. To create an ID style rule, click the **Selector Type** field box and select the **ID** option.

3. In the **Selector Name** field box type **#price** (remember to enter the pound sign first) and click **OK**.

4. With the style assistant, establish a series of characteristics for the text affected by the advanced rule. Open the **Font Family** menu and select font combination, **Arial, Helvetica, sans-serif.**

Note that the style rule is created within the selected style sheet.

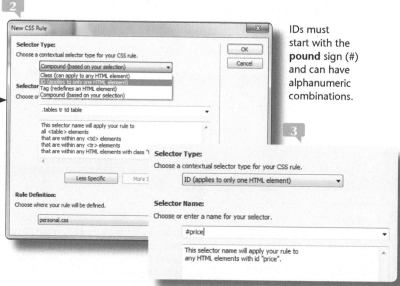

IDs must start with the **pound** sign (#) and can have alphanumeric combinations.

138

063

5. In **Font Size**, select **12**.

6. Click the arrow in **Font-weight** and select **bold**.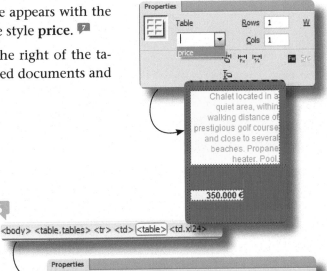

7. Access the **Background** category and select a light yellow color as the background color.

8. In the **Border** category select **solid** for border style, **1 pixel** for width value, and intense green for color.

9. Click **OK** when the style properties have been established.

10. When certain elements are selected, a field box at the beginning of the **Properties** panel pops up displaying a name that changes according to the element selected. In the tag selector, click **<table>**.

11. In this case, the field box mentioned above appears with the name **Table**. Open the menu and select the style **price**.

12. Click on the background of the page, to the right of the table, save all the changes made on the opened documents and close them.

Remember that not all the elements of a page can be identified.

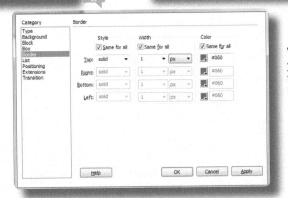

Identifiers can be modified through programming. The style rule will be applied to the element identified with the advanced rule name.

With the table selected, you can apply the identifier from the ID field in the Properties panel.

Using frames

DREAMWEAVER CS6 INTRODUCES A NEW WAY of creating pages with frames. The predefined frameset folder has been eliminated from the program, just as the corresponding command in the Insert panel has also been eliminated, which means that currently, framesets can be created only from scratch. In other words, to insert single and nested frames in pages, you now need to access the Frame submenu in the Insert menu. The insertion of a frame means the automatic generation of two HTML pages, the one storing the structure of the various frames and the one created as the source for the inserted frame.

1. Begin by creating a new blank page and attach the **colors3.css** style page; you already know that you can do this from the **CSS styles** panel.

2. To create the frames, open the **Insert** menu, click **HTML** and click the command **Frames**.

3. The list includes options to create single and nested frames. Select the **Top** option.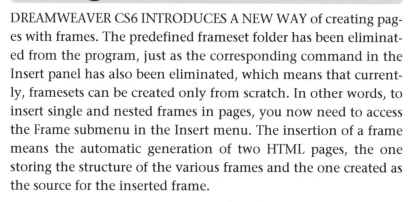

4. The new frame appears above the page. The program automatically generates a temporary file, a blank page as the source for the new frame. Click the top frame and type the word **Browser**.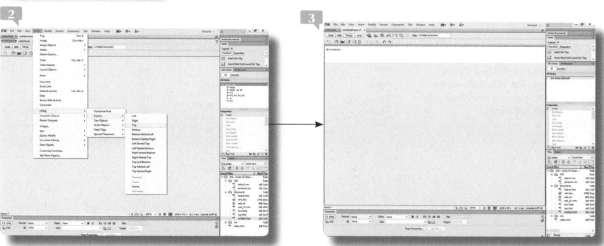

064

5. Open the **File** menu and click **Save All**.

6. The insertion of the frame has generated a page that controls the structure, the framesets themselves. This is the first page that needs to be saved. Select the **documents** folder, type the word **set** and click **Save**.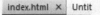

7. The program will now ask to store the first page created in the exercise, the one attached to the **colors3.css** page. In the **File name** field box type the word **contact** and click **Save**.

8. Now save the file corresponding to the top frame. Enter the word **nothing** in the **File name** field and click **Save**.

9. Once the various documents have been saved, 5 click to close the page.

10. Access the **Files** panel and double-click the **contact.html** page. Verify that the page opens independently and then close it.

11. Notice that opening the page that stores the frame structures means opening all the pages contained in the set. Go to the **Files** panel and click the **set.html** document.

12. Open the **Modify** menu, display the **Frameset** submenu and select **Split Frame Right**. 6

13. The top frame is now split into two frames. 7 Close the **set.html** page without saving the changes made to any of the pages.

IMPORTANT

Dreamweaver automatically assigns a default file name, Untitled Frameset, followed by the corresponding number, to the newly created set of frames.

> index.html × Untit

The program highlights the corresponding frame in the document's window.

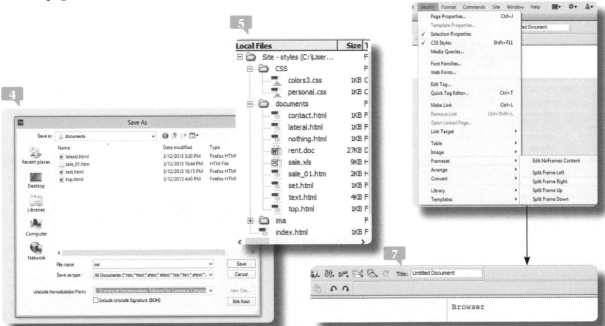

Browser

Setting frameset properties

FRAMES SPLIT A BROWSER WINDOW into various regions, each of which can show a different HTML document. To use pages with frames you need to create a set of frames, meaning an HTML file that defines the design and properties of a group of frames. This file does not include the HTML content displayed in the browser.

1. In this exercise you will complete the frame page generated in the previous exercise by creating a new frame and setting the characteristics. Double-click the **set.html** page in the **Files** panel.

2. The new document, consisting of two frames, opens. Click the larger frame, the bottom frame, display the **Modify** panel, click **Frameset** and select **Split Frame Right**.

3. The page is now divided in two columns and one row. In the **Properties** panel select **Borders** and click **Yes**.

4. The borders of a frame can be visible or hidden. Click the arrow point in the **Border Color** field box and select a dark green tone.

Any set containing different frame numbers in different rows or columns requires a nested frameset.

065

5. The border separating the three frames immediately turns dark green. Enter the value **3** in the **Border width** field and press **Enter**.

6. Frames can have fixed or relative dimensions. In this case, the first row of the selected set has a default height of 80 pixels. Insert the number **220** in the **value** field box of the row and press **Enter**.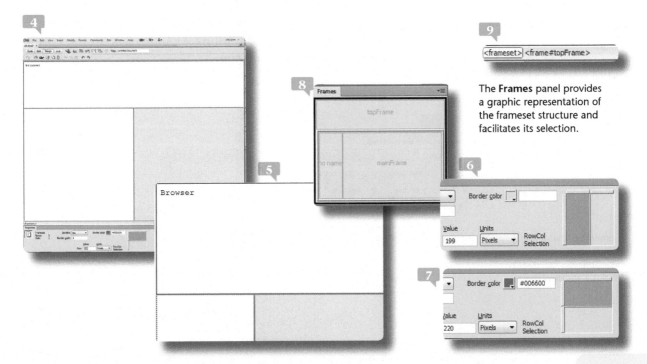

7. Next, click the vertical border separating the two bottom frames and, while continuing to press the mouse button, drag it to the left to decrease the width.

8. Verify that the **RowCol Selection** graph in the Properties panel changes according to the border selected on the page. In this way you can control the available framesets. Click the horizontal border and see how the graph changes.

9. Open the **Window** menu and select the **Frames** option to open the Frames panel and verify the structure of the page with frames and its denominations.

10. Click the **topFrame** section to select the top frame.

11. In the tag selector select the **frameset** tag, display the **File** menu and click **Save Frameset** to save.

The HTML **frame** tag corresponds to one frame and the **frameset** tag corresponds to a set of frames.

The **Frames** panel provides a graphic representation of the frameset structure and facilitates its selection.

Assigning a source to display in frames

THE MOST COMMON USE OF FRAMES IS FOR NAVIGATION. A set of frames includes one frame containing a navigation bar and another frame displaying the pages containing the main content. An advantage of using frames is that the visitor's browser doesn't need to reload the navigation graphics again for each page, since the document containing them remains loaded. However, not all navigators are compatible with their use and some visitors may encounter difficulties when browsing the pages.

1. To create any given set of frames, the program generates blank pages. The first page, which contains the structure of the frames and was previously saved with the name **set**, is the actual set of frames, in other words, the HTML page containing the structure of the various frames. Each of the other two generated pages corresponds to the frames contained in the set. In the **Frames** panel click the **topFrame** box.

2. The top frame is linked to the **nothing.html** file, as you can see in the **Src** section of the **Properties** panel. The name of the frame functions as an identifier and can be modified from the **Properties** panel. The identifier permits the control of the frame through programming. Double-click on the **Frame name** and type the word **top**.

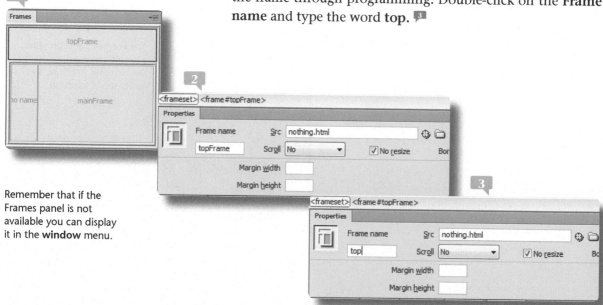

Remember that if the Frames panel is not available you can display it in the **window** menu.

144

3. Click the folder icon of the **Src** field 4 and, in the **Select HTML File** dialog box, double-click the **documents** folder and double-click the **top.html** page. 5

4. The initial page will be automatically deleted and, instead, the frame will contain the page of the selected site. 6 Select the left frame, currently named **no name**, by clicking this term in the **Frames** panel. 7

5. Click the **Frame name** field box and type the word **lateral**. 8

6. Repeat the steps above, delete, in this case, the temporary file created by the program for this second frame, including the content in the **lateral** page of the **documents** folder. 9

7. Select the right frame by clicking **mainFrame** in the **Frames** panel, name it **content** and add as a source the **text** file in the **documents** folder. 10

8. Open the **lateral** page from the **Files** panel.

9. Click **Page Properties**, the **Appearance (HTML)** category, and select a background color.

10. Close the **lateral** page and click **Yes** to save the changes.

11. Notice that the change of color has been updated in **set.html**. 11 Press the key combination **Ctrl + S** to save the changes.

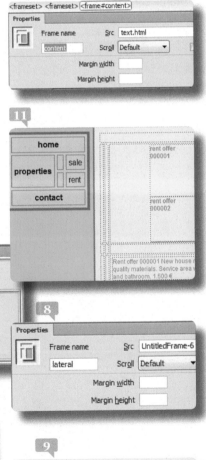

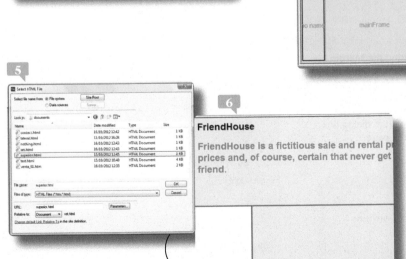

Changing frame properties

THE NAME, APPEARANCE OF BORDERS, thickness, color, or class style characteristics are some of the frame properties that can be modified. The Scroll drop-down menu controls whether the frame scroll bar is displayed or not. If you select the Yes option, the scroll bar pops up, if on the contrary you select No, they do not, and the Auto option means that the scroll bar appears when necessary. The No Resize option prevents visitors from dragging the frame borders to resize the frame on the browser. The Margin height and width fields set the distance in pixels between the frame borders and the content.

1. The top frame of the **set.html** page occupies the first row of the main frameset. Select the **top** frame by clicking its name in the **Frames** panel.

2. Setting a fixed margin height cancels the frame's scroll bar, which is why the option **No** appears in the **Scroll** field box. The **Margin width** field box determines the space separating the frame borders and the content, click the field and type 110 and press **Enter**.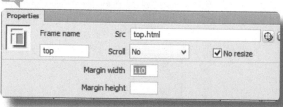

3. The **Margin height** value determines the space between the top and bottom frame borders and the content. Enter the number 10 in the field box and press **Enter**.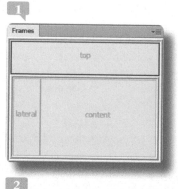

Setting the **Margin width** and **height** of a frame is not the same as defining the margins in the Properties dialog box of the page.

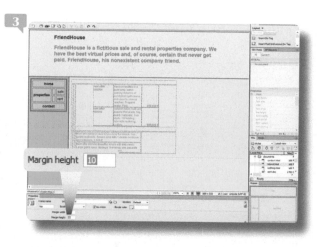

067

4. Go to the **Frames** panel and select the frame named **lateral**.

5. Click the **Margin height** field box and enter the value **10** and press **Enter**.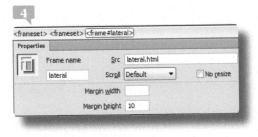

6. The third frame, named **content**, is specified to have relative sizes, since the column containing it does not have a fixed width. Select this frame from the **Frames** panel.

7. Setting the **Scroll** value to **Default** doesn't set a value for the corresponding attribute, allowing each navigator to use its default value. Display the **Scroll** menu and select **Auto**. 5

8. The **Auto** option is recommended for frames without fixed dimensions, since the scroll bars will appear only when necessary, with the horizontal and vertical bars functioning independently. Enter the number **7** in the **Margin height** field and click **Enter**. 6

9. Preview the set of frames, save the changes made and click **F12**.

10. Each frame has a corresponding source page. Resize the window until the corresponding scroll bars appear. 7

11. Just as specified, only the bottom frames have scroll bars to access the entire content. Click the bottom of the **vertical scroll bar** and, to finish, close the browser and the **set.html** page storing the frame structure.

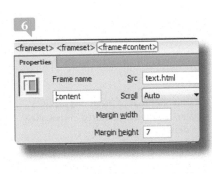

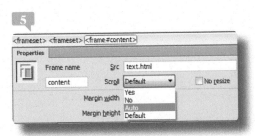

The **Yes** option displays both frame scroll bars, regardless of whether the content is entirely visible or not, and the option **No** hides the scroll bars.

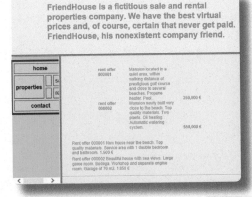

Inserting image placeholders

IMPORTANT

The **Name** field in the Placeholder dialog box is optional. You can leave it blank if you prefer no tags. In case you complete it, remember that the name must begin with a letter and can contain only letters and numbers. Spaces and high ASCII characters are not accepted.

AN IMAGE PLACEHOLDER is a temporary graphic used until the image is ready to be added to the web page. Before publishing the site you should replace all the placeholders with web-friendly image files. Dreamweaver facilitates the creation of the final image from the inserted placeholder. Click the Create button in the Properties panel. The placeholder opens Fireworks, if the program is available, with a blank document of the same size as the placeholder. In the source field select any image contained in the site.

1. Before you start, go to the download page and copy files **rent_01.gif**, **rent_02.gif**, **rent_03.gif**, **FriendHouse.gif**, **go_01.gif**, **go_02.gif**, **s_01.gif**, **s_02.gif** and **s_03.gif** to the **styles** site's images folder. Next, go to the **Files** panel and open the **index.htm** page also from the site. 1
2. Insert a placeholder in a new paragraph at the end of the page. Click at the end of the word **FriendHouse** and click **Enter** to insert a carriage return.
3. Open the **Insert** menu to display the **Image Objects** submenu and select **Image Placeholder.** 2
4. The **Image Placeholder** box determines the object's proper-

Remember that to insert images on a page, they must be stored in that site's folders.

1

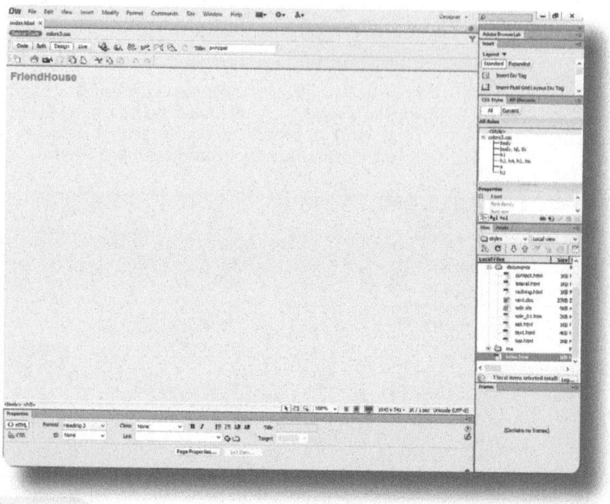

2

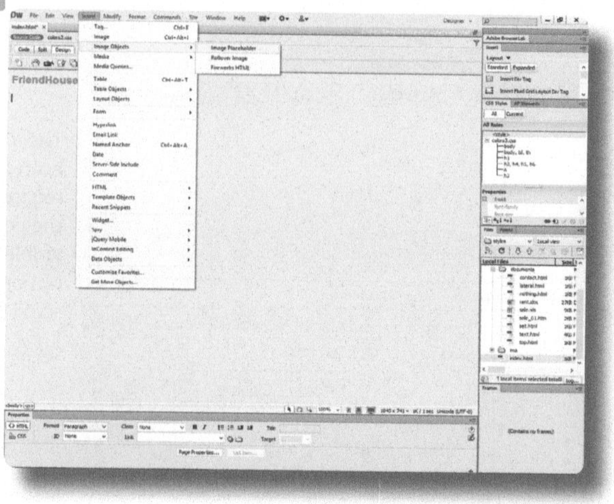

068

ties before inserting it on the page. In the **Name** field type the term **logo**.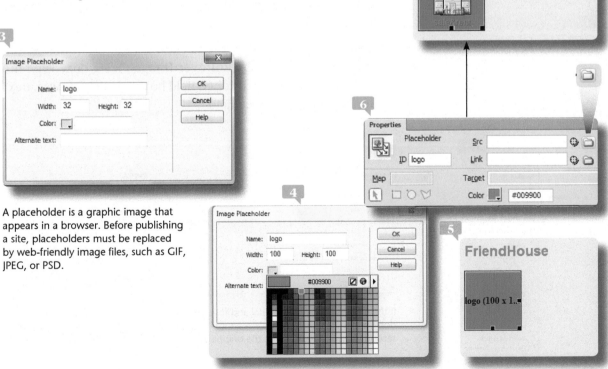

5. The main function of the image placeholder is to develop the structure of the page, allowing space for the missing image so that it can be easily inserted on the page without disturbing the rest of the layout. The graphic replacing the placeholder has a width and height of **100** pixels. Enter these values in the **Width** and **Height** field boxes.

6. Click the arrow point in the **Color** field and select an intense green tone from the color chart.

7. In the **Alternate Text** field box you can enter a text describing the image for text-only browser users. Click **OK**.

8. The image placeholder is added to the page. Use the **Properties** panel to modify attributes and select additional options. Use one of the files stored in the **styles** site at the beginning of the exercise. Click the folder icon in the **Src** field, open the **ima** folder, select the **FriendHouse.gif** document and click **Accept**.

9. The selected file replaces the placeholder, and the **Properties** panel shows the final image. Click the **Save** icon to save the changes.

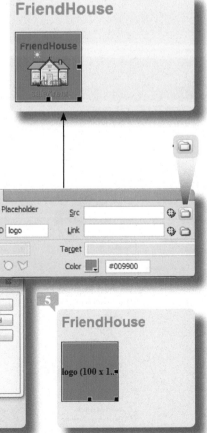

FriendHouse

A placeholder is a graphic image that appears in a browser. Before publishing a site, placeholders must be replaced by web-friendly image files, such as GIF, JPEG, or PSD.

Creating rollover images

A ROLLOVER IS AN IMAGE THAT WHEN VIEWED in a browser changes WHEN the pointer moves over it. To create a rollover you need two files: the original image file, the one that is visible when the page is initially uploaded, and the rollover image file, the one displayed when the mouse rolls over the main image. Both need to have identical width and height dimensions. The Insert Rollover Image dialog box simplifies the selection of these files. The Preload Rollover Image box, indicating that the secondary image will be uploaded in the browser's cache when accessing the page, is enabled by default.

1. Add a carriage return after the GIF image inserted in the **index.htm** page.

2. The **Insert** menu simplifies the inclusion of the various objects of the image on the page, but there is an alternative to inserting this type of object. Select the **Common** category in the **Insert** panel.

3. Click the arrow in the **Images** icon and select **Rollover Image**.

4. You can assign an ID to the image object in the **Image name** field box in the **Insert Rollover Image** dialog box. Type the word **enter** in the mentioned field box and click **Browse**, next to the **Original image** field.

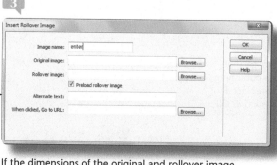

The Insert Rollover Image dialog box permits inserting a link, as well as including alternative text for users of text-only browser.

If the dimensions of the original and rollover image don't match, Dreamweaver resizes automatically the secondary image to adjust to the original.

069

5. The selected file is the image that will be initially inserted on the page. Locate and select **go_01**, and click **OK**.

6. The path to the secondary image must be inserted in the **Rollover image** field box. Click the **Browse** button to the right of the box, locate and select the file **go_02**, and click **OK**.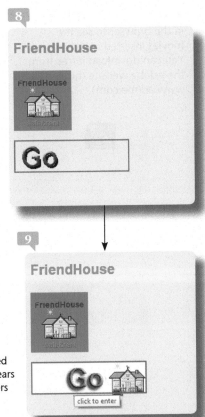

7. The **Preload Rollover Image** box is enabled by default so that the secondary image will be uploaded to the browser's cache when accessing the page and will appear faster when the visitor rolls the mouse over the original image. Enter the text **click to enter** in the **Alternate Text** field box and click **OK**.

8. The alternative text is a description of the image for text-only browser users. Some browsers, such as Internet Explorer, display this text in tag form when placing the mouse pointer over the object. Select the image and click **Split** to show the code.

9. When the image is selected it will show the code corresponding to the image. Select the **alt** text and replace it with **title**.

10. Save the changes made in the page and preview it in your web browser.

11. The rollover image shows the original image. Place the mouse on the original so that the secondary image appears and, after verifying that everything functions correctly, close the navigator and the **index.htm** page.

Notice that the inserted **Alternative Text** appears when the mouse hovers over the image.

151

Adding Flash movies

ADOBE FLASH LETS YOU ADD ANIMATION AND VIDEOS to web pages that can vary from small animated vector graphics to complex web applications. Flash generates various types of files called movies. The .fla extension files are editable but cannot be inserted in pages and, the web-optimized-and-compressed SWF files, although not editable in Flash, can be inserted and visualized in navigators and Dreamweaver. When you insert an SWF file, use the Properties panel to assign an ID to the object, as well as modify the dimensions of the page area, or placeholder, targeted for the movie, and select the corresponding source file.

1. Go to the download section of our website and copy the **media** folder to the **styles** site. In this exercise you will insert a Flash movie in the **top.htm** page. So, open the page and click the start of the second paragraph. 🔲

2. The folder you just copied contains two Flash files, with the same name but different format, called **FriendHouse**. The first file is an editable .fla extension file, and the second is a .swf extension file, a compressed version of that same file. Flash movies are multimedia objects. Open the **Insert** menu, click **Media** and select **SWF**. 🔲

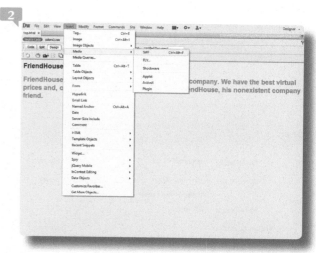

070

3. The **Select File** dialog box opens to select the Flash file you wish to insert. Only .swf extension files can be inserted because they are the only ones that can be seen in browsers Locate and open the **media** folder, select the **FriendHouse.swf** file and click **OK**.

4. Automatically a Flash placeholder appears on the document window. 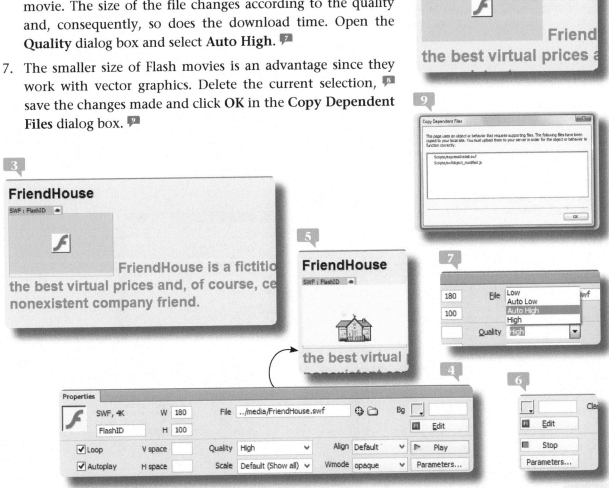 The path of the inserted file is stored in the **File** field box in the **Properties** panel, where you can verify the movie shows the .swf extension that corresponds to Flash output files. In the Properties panel, click **Play**.

5. The movie consists of a simple animation that loops back. The **Loop** verification checkbox determines this behavior. Click **Autoplay** to automatically play the movie when the browser loads the page containing it. Click **Stop**.

6. The **Properties** panel also lets you select the quality of the movie. The size of the file changes according to the quality and, consequently, so does the download time. Open the **Quality** dialog box and select **Auto High**.

7. The smaller size of Flash movies is an advantage since they work with vector graphics. Delete the current selection, save the changes made and click **OK** in the **Copy Dependent Files** dialog box.

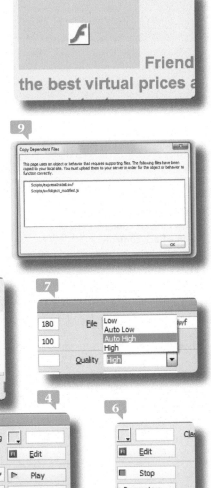

Inserting Flash Videos

THE .FLV EXTENSION FLASH FILES are video files containing audio and video code data delivered through the Flash player. It's easy to add videos to pages with Dreamweaver by using a specific function you can find in the Media submenu of the Insert menu, or the Media command of the Insert panel.

1. Place the edit cursor on any empty area of the page, open the **Insert** menu and on the **Media** command select **FLV**.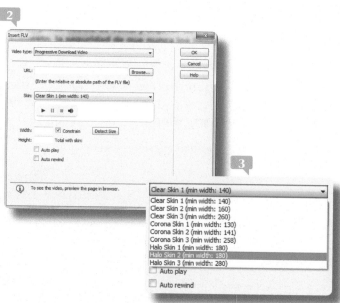

2. The **Insert FLV** dialog box determines the properties of the file. In the **Video Type** field, keep **Progressive Download Video** selected so that the FLV file can initiate even before the download is finished. To locate and select the file in question click **Browse**.

3. Access the content of the **media** folder, select the sample file **Planets.flv** and click **OK**.

4. In the **Skin** field box you can define the appearance of the video component. You can see a preview of the selection below the pop-up menu. Click the arrow button and select **Halo skin 2 (min width: 180)**.

When inserting an FLV video in Dreamweaver, the program inserts an SWF component that shows the file content and a set of **playback controls**.

154

5. In the **Width** and **Height** field specify the dimensions in pixels for the movie. For Dreamweaver to calculate the exact file dimensions, click **Detect Size**.

6. The **Auto play** option determines if the file will play when the web page opens, and the **Auto rewind** determines if the playback control returns to the start when the video finishes. Disable both options. Click **OK.**

7. The object corresponding to the FLV file is automatically added to the page. Notice that a video player SWF file and a video SWF file have been created to display the video content in the page. These files are stored the site's folder where the video is stored, which in this case is the **media** folder. Save the changes and preview the page in your web browser.

8. Since you haven't selected autoplay, click **Play** in the video play control to start it.

9. Close the browser in the **Title Bar.**

10. To finish the exercise, click **Delete** to remove the inserted movie and save the changes made.

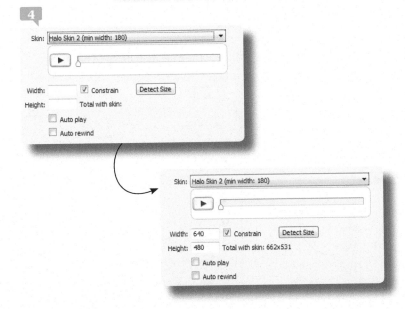

Inserting Flash buttons

DREAMWEAVER LETS YOU INSERT BUTTONS created in Flash and exported in SWF format. Buttons are elements that describe an interactive behavior activated when the mouse rolls over or clicks it.

IMPORTANT

When inserting a Flash button in Dreamweaver, the animation, links, and actions must be predetermined in Flash.

1. The **media** folder you downloaded from our website and stored in the styles folder contains a file named **button.swf**. 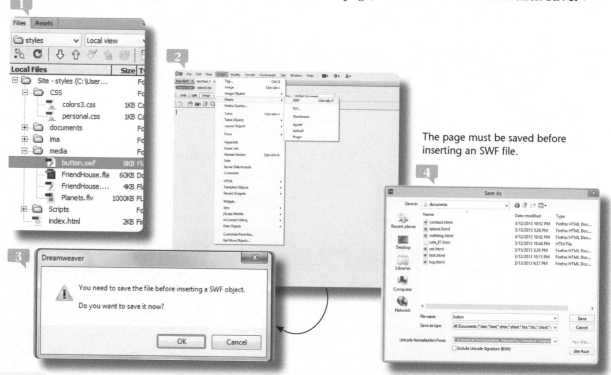 This file contains a button created with Flash and exported in .swf that you can insert in Dreamweaver and activate. Display the **Insert** menu, select the **Media** command and click the **SWF** option.

2. If you haven't saved the page you are working on, a warning dialog box telling you to save will pop up on the screen before you can insert another element. Click the **OK** button in this box.

3. In the **Save As** window select the **documents** site folder as the place for the new page, rename it **button** and click **Save**.

The page must be saved before inserting an SWF file.

156

4. The **Select SWF** dialog box opens. Locate and select the **button.swf** file. Click **OK**.

5. Notice that the file has been added to the selected page and the information has been updated in the **Properties** panel. Click **Play** in the **Properties** panel to see the movie content.

6. Notice that you can see the button correctly and the animation is functioning correctly. Place the mouse pointer on the center button and click it.

7. Save the changes and then verify how they will look in the browser.

8. After saving the changes, click **F12** to preview and click the button to verify the animation works correctly.

9. Close the web browser and **button.html**.

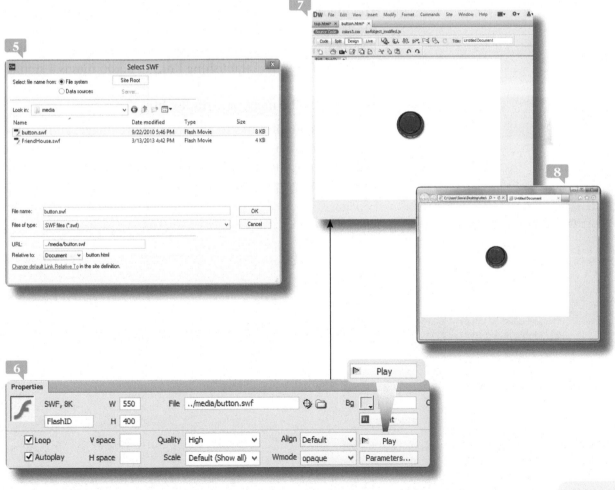

Linking Sounds

ESTABLISHING LINKS TO AUDIO FILES IS A SIMPLE and efficient way of adding sounds to a web page and letting users decide whether or not they listen. If you click the link, after the page is loaded in the browser, you automatically open the file linked to the program pre-defined for that purpose. There are many audio formats: WAV and AIF provide excellent audio quality but their large size increases the downloading time. Before choosing a format and method to add sound, consider the following: purpose, type of user targeted, size, and file quality. The MP3 and Real compressed formats offer a good quality-size relation, but visitors need the corresponding application for it.

1. The **media** folder in the **styles** site contains two WAV format files ■ (the folder is located in the download section of our website). Inserting either type of file on the page increases downloading time. Establishing links to audio files is a simple and efficient way to add sound to a page. In the **Files** panel double-click the main page, **index.htm**. ■

2. Pages can contain links to all sorts of files: image, audio, video, text documents, etc. Include text at the end of the page to link it to an audio file. Click the word **Go,** click the **Enter** key to add a paragraph, type the word **sound** and select it. ■

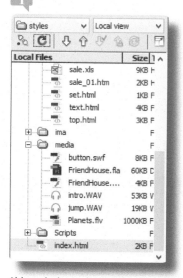

Adding audio files through links lets visitors choose whether they want to hear them or not.

Although the audio quality of .wav extension files is good, their large size is a disadvantage.

073

3. In the exercises explaining how to establish links, you saw how the program lets you use different options to create a link. In this case use the field corresponding to the **Properties** panel. Click the icon in the folder of the field **Link**. 4

4. Select the file to be linked. Open the **media** folder, select the **intro** file and, to create a permanent link, click **OK**.

5. The route to the selected file is included in the **Link** field of the **Properties** panel. To verify the correct functioning, save the changes made on the page and preview it in the browser.

6. The sound doesn't play automatically, you need to click the **sound** link; do it now. 5

7. The CS6 version uses Adobe Audition as the player and editor for sound files, 6 but you can use other players to execute files with this type of format. 7 Close the player and the browser to finish this exercise.

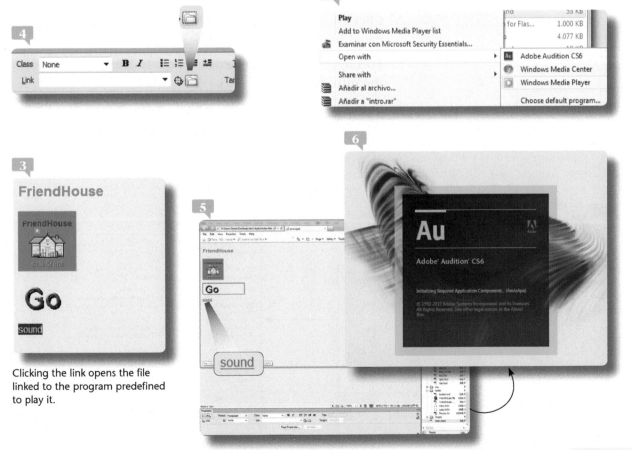

Clicking the link opens the file linked to the program predefined to play it.

Inserting sounds

IMPORTANT

Shockwave is a compressed format that allows Director-generated files to download quickly and play in the more common browsers. An Applet is a small software application that normally has a Java program language. The Parameters command lets you create page ID controllers; ActiveX connectors make Internet navigation comparable to a CD-ROM, letting the user listen to music, see animations and video clips, and interact with the program.

IN ADDITION TO FLASH MOVIES, Dreamweaver lets you insert other multimedia objects: Shockwave movies, Java applets, parameters, and Active X controls and plug-ins. All of these objects can be inserted through options in the Menu Bar or the media command in the Insert panel. The program lets you insert sounds directly into the pages, but it only works if the users have the corresponding plug-in. To insert the sound, you need to select it when you click the plug-in command. Once inserted on the page, the sound is represented by a placeholder in the document window.

1. In this exercise you will insert sounds directly in the page. Delete the hypertext linked to the sound file inserted in the previous exercise.

2. Click the arrow point of the **Media** command in the **Insert** panel and click the **Plugin** option.

3. This opens the **Select File** dialog box. Locate and select again the **intro.wav** file and click **OK.**

4. It is especially important which audio format is selected when the file is embedded, since the page increases its size

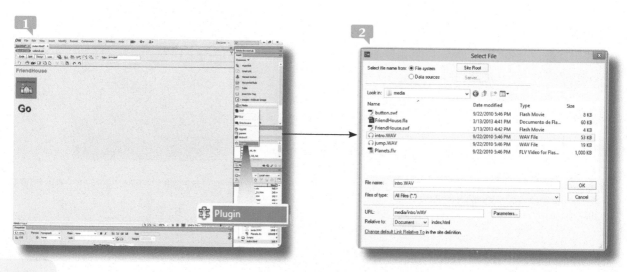

proportionately and, therefore, the download time increases. Click **Ctrl + S** to save the changes made.

5. Preview the page to verify the result. Click **F12**.

6. The sound plays automatically when the page is loaded in the browser. The point at where the sound was embedded the typical **Play image** button appears, click it.

7. The button is part of the player, program, or plug-in that remains embedded in the page to play the sound. Click the cross button in the browser **Title Bar**.

8. The embedded sound object appears as a placeholder. The **W** and **H** field in the **Properties** panel modifies the size of the object. In this case delete the player from the page so that the user can't control the playing of the embedded audio file. Double-click the **W** field, enter the value **0** and click **Enter**. Repeat the same for the **H** field.

9. Preview the page one more time to verify the effect of the modifications. Click **Ctrl + S** to save the changes and then click **F12**.

10. The sound plays when the page is loaded, but in this case there are no controls that allow the user to replay the sounds. Close the browser to finish.

074

IMPORTANT

The URL field in the Properties panel lets you specify the complete URL for the site from where users can download the corresponding plug-in to play the sound in the browser. If the user doesn't have the plug-in, the browser will try to unload it from that address.

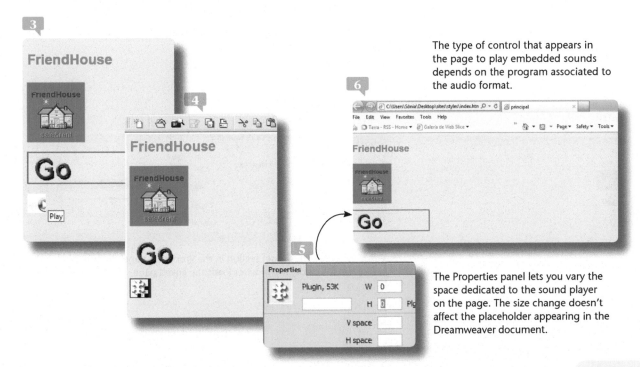

The type of control that appears in the page to play embedded sounds depends on the program associated to the audio format.

The Properties panel lets you vary the space dedicated to the sound player on the page. The size change doesn't affect the placeholder appearing in the Dreamweaver document.

Linking pages and modifying how they load

BY DEFAULT, A LINKED PAGE loads in the same browser window as the link, replacing it (the _self option). However, Dreamweaver lets you assign other targets for links. The _blank option loads the page in another browser window. The _top and _parent options have to do with frames: the first option indicates that the linked page loads in the current browser window, removing all frames, and the second option loads the linked page in the parent frameset of the frame containing the link, replacing the whole set.

1. The **index.htm** page contains a replacement image with the text **Go**. Click it.

2. Link the page to the frameset created in the previous exercises. Click the folder icon of the **Link** box in the **Properties** panel.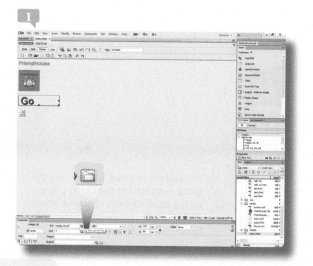

3. In the **Select File** dialog box, locate and select **set.html**.

4. Loading the set in the browser affects the other pages in the set's frames. Display **Target** in the Properties panel.

5. The current page doesn't have frames, so there are only the four traditional targets. Select **_self**.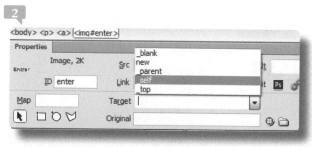

6. Clicking on the image replacement loads the set of frames in

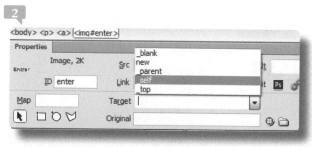

The Target section in the Properties panel determines how the browser loads the linked page.

the browser's window. Go to the **Files** panel and open **set.html**.

7. Select the word **home** located in the table in the **lateral** frame, on the lower left side of the set. **3**

8. Click the folder icon in the **Link** section of the **Properties** panel and locate and select the **index.htm** page.

9. Click the arrow button **Target**.

10. In addition to the traditional options, you'll see a list of names of the frames that make up the set. If you set **_top**, the main page replaces the entire set of frames. **4**

11. Double-click the word **contact**, located in the last cell of the **lateral** frame table. **5**

12. Click the **Link** folder icon, and locate and select the **contact** page. **6**

13. Display the **Target** menu in the **Properties** pane and select **content**. **7**

14. Click **Control** and continue pressing while clicking the cell containing **rent offert 000001**.

15. Link it to the **sale_01** page and, in the **Target** section, select **_blank**.

16. To finish, open the **File** menu and click **Save All**.

IMPORTANT

The Modify menu, through the options in the Link Target submenu, establishes targets. In addition to the accessible options available in the Target drop-down menu, the submenu has access to the Establish Target dialog box. In addition to the accessible options, the Target submenu lets you access the Establish Target dialog box where you can type the target directly.

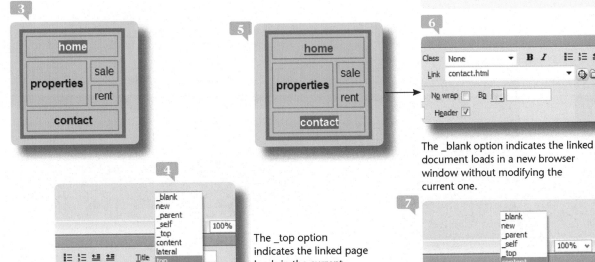

The _blank option indicates the linked document loads in a new browser window without modifying the current one.

The _top option indicates the linked page loads in the current browser window, removing all frames.

Creating named anchors

NAMED ANCHORS link a specific section of a document to sections of the same, or another, document. Anchors are particularly useful when we want to link parts of a long document instead of scrolling back and forth.

1. In our download section locate the **odyssey.html** document and open it in Dreamweaver.

2. There is an index at the top and long text divided into four sections. The objective of the exercise is to jump directly from the index to the corresponding section. Use the vertical scroll bar to move the text to the start of Book II.

3. Place the cursor at the end of the title, open the **Insert** menu and select **Named Anchor**.

4. In the **Anchor Name** box, type **Book2** and click **OK**.

5. Insert an anchored-shaped icon at the point where the edit cursor is. Go back to the index and select the second line.

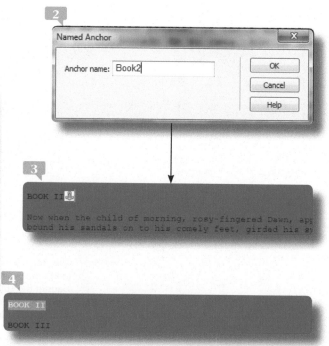

The key combination Ctrl + Alt + A accesses the Named Anchor dialog box.

076

6. In the **Properties** panel, and with the second index line selected, type **#Book2** in the **Link** box, without forgetting to enter the pound sign.

7. Place the edit cursor at the end of the title, use the **Named Anchor** command in the **Insert** panel 🔲 to insert a new anchor where the edit cursor is and name it **start**. 🔲

8. The new anchor 🔲 is the point to where each **jump to start** link inserted in the page will return to. Scroll to the end of the first text block, select it and type **#start** in the Link box of the **Properties** panel. 🔲

9. Verify the anchors work correctly. Save the changes made and click **F12** to see the page in the browser.

10. The second index title is underlined, indicating it's a link; click it. 🔲

11. The page automatically jumps to the beginning of Book II, where the first anchor was inserted. Now click the text **jump to start**.

12. After verifying both anchors work correctly, close the navigator.

13. You may repeat the operation as many times as you want, until you link each index line to its corresponding text.

Notice that the named anchor link shows up just as any other web link, with the link text underlined and in blue.

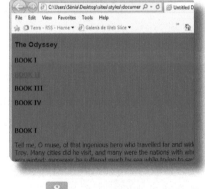

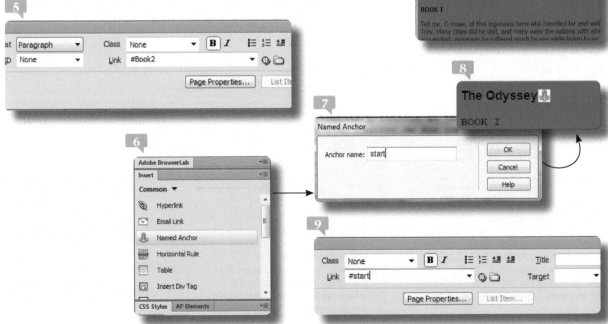

Inserting AP elements

DREAMWEAVER LETS YOU INSERT AP ELEMENTS, before called layers, to simplify page design. An AP element is an HTML page element that can be placed anywhere in the document and, in turn, can contain the same elements as an HTML document. When an AP element is inserted, Dreamweaver inserts the HTML div tag in the body of the page. The **div** tag is a block level element that permits the creation of blocks in a document having differentiated content. You can use the options in the Menu Bar to insert AP elements directly or draw them by clicking the Draw AP Div button in the Design category of the Insert toolbar.

1. Open the **contact.html** page in the **styles** site file from the **Files** panel.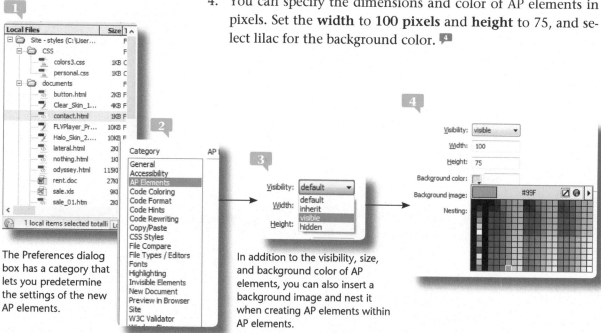

2. Before inserting the first AP element, modify the default settings. Open the **Edit** menu, click **Preferences** and, in the dialog box, enable the **AP Elements** category.

3. AP Elements can be visible or hidden. Open the **Visibility** box and select **visible**.

4. You can specify the dimensions and color of AP elements in pixels. Set the **width** to **100 pixels** and **height** to 75, and select lilac for the background color.

The Preferences dialog box has a category that lets you predetermine the settings of the new AP elements.

In addition to the visibility, size, and background color of AP elements, you can also insert a background image and nest it when creating AP elements within AP elements.

077

5. The other options are for background images and to determine if an AP element that is drawn form a starting point that is within the limits of an already existing AP element should be a nested AP element. Click **OK**.

6. Open the **Insert** menu, click **Layout Objects** and select the **AP Div** command. **5**

7. The basic AP element is inserted at the beginning of the page. **6** Open the **Insert** menu, click **Image** and, in the **ima** folder, locate and select the **min_v01** file and click **OK**. **7**

8. Click **Enter** to add a paragraph, type the word **sale 8** and click to the right of the AP element to delete the selection. Next, draw a second AP element. To do this, click **Ctrl + Alt + G** to display the first grid.

9. Select the Layout category in the **Insert** panel, click **Draw AP Div 9** and drag to trace a slightly wider div element to the right of the already existing one. **10**

10. Repeat the same steps to insert the **min_a01** image in the new div tag.

11. Type the word **rent** below the element **11** and, to finish, click **Ctrl + S** to save.

IMPORTANT

You can also display a grid in Dreamweaver from the **View** menu. To do this, select **Show Grid** in the **Grid** drop-down menu.

Show Grid	Ctrl+Alt+G
Snap To Grid	Ctrl+Alt+Shift+G
Grid Settings...	

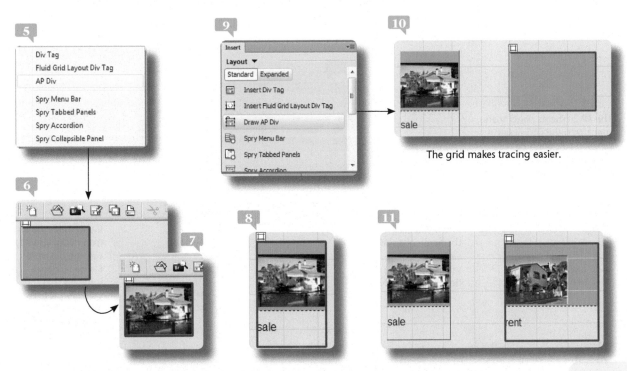

The grid makes tracing easier.

Changing AP Elements properties

USE THE AP ELEMENTS PANEL to avoid overlapping, change visibility or select one or more elements. AP elements are listed by name in descending order. In the HTML code, the Z index of the AP elements determines the order in which they are drawn in a browser. The Properties panel lets you modify the stacking order and control the dimensions and page placement. You can select AP elements from the AP Elements panel or in the document window. You can also specify properties for multiple AP elements in the Properties panel.

1. Click the tab in the **AP Elements** panel.

2. The first AP element inserted is positioned at the end of the list, while the most recent one is in first place. Click **apDiv1**, type the word **sale** and click **Enter**.

3. To hide the **sale** element, double-click the eye icon.

4. The **AP Elements** panel's visibility column displays several icons according to the state of the element: an open eye indicates it is visible, and a closed eye indicates it is hidden. Click the **sale** element's icon to redisplay.

IMPORTANT

The Overflow option in the lower part of the Properties panel determines how the AP element appears in the browser when the content exceeds the specified size, and Clip defines its visible area.

The AP Elements panel shares space with the CSS Styles panel. If you don't have it, remember that you can access it from the Window menu.

When you click the name of an AP element, you are selecting it in the document window.

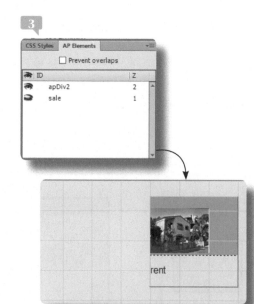

If you don't see an icon in the visibility column of the AP Elements panel, it means that the visibility property is inherited from the parent or principal AP Element.

078

5. Select the **sale** object in the AP Elements panel.

6. In the document's window click the upper left corner of the element and drag all the way to the upper left-hand corner of the selected element. 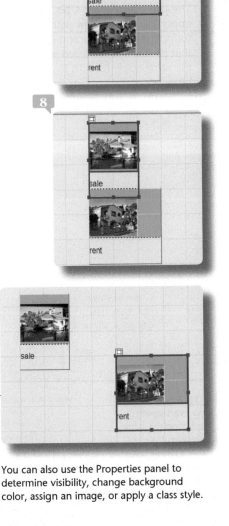 Deselect the element by clicking on the page.

7. The numbers in the **Z** column of the **AP Elements** panel indicate the position of the different elements. Double-click the column value in the **sale** element, enter the number **3** and press **Enter**.

8. Click the name of the second **AP Element**, double-click the **CSS-P Element** in the Properties panel, type the word **rent** and click **Enter**.

9. Enter **400px** in the L box and **150px** in the T box to change the placement of the element.

10. Click, in the document window, on the **sale** element and enter **400px** in the L box and press **Enter**.

11. Click center-right of the selected AP element and drag until the width is the same as the **rent** element.

12. To finish the exercise, disable the grid and save the changes.

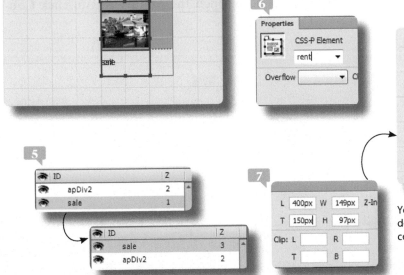

You can also use the Properties panel to determine visibility, change background color, assign an image, or apply a class style.

Converting AP Elements into tables

THE AP ELEMENTS OFFER GREAT FLEXIBILITY when it comes to placing the content of a document, but only the newer browser versions can support them. The Convert AP DIVS to Table command permits the automatic use of GIF transparencies to ensure that the resulting table has the same column width in all browsers.

1. Browser versions before Internet Explorer 4.0 and Netscape Navigator 4.0 can't show layers, while version 4.0 navigators don't show AP elements in a coherent fashion. To solve this problem, open the **Modify** menu, click **Convert** and then select **AP Divs to Table.** 🔲

2. The **Most accurate** option in the **Convert Divs to Table** dialog box determines the creation of a cell for each AP element and the necessary additional cells to respect the distance between elements. Select **Center on page** and **Prevent overlaps** and click **Ok.** 🔲

3. The program detects elements overlapping. Click **OK** in the alert pop-up menu. 🔲

4. To solve overlapping, select the **rent** element and enter the value **200px** in the T field box in the **Properties** panel.

5. Press the **Shift** key and, while holding it down, click the **sale** element to select both, open the **Modify** menu, click **Con-**

Tables to AP Divs...
AP Divs to Table...

This way there is no overlapping, ensuring the table presents the content of each table in independent cells, regardless of the original position of the elements.

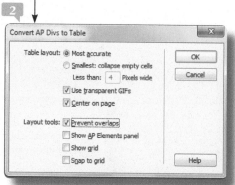

Convert AP Divs to Table

Table layout: ● Most accurate
○ Smallest: collapse empty cells
Less than: 4 Pixels wide
☑ Use transparent GIFs
☑ Center on page
Layout tools: ☑ Prevent overlaps
☐ Show AP Elements panel
☐ Show grid
☐ Snap to grid

OK   Cancel   Help

Overlapping AP Elements Detected

This file cannot be converted because it contains overlapping AP divs.

'sale' overlaps with 'rent'.

OK

079

vert, select **AP Divs to Table** and click **OK** in the conversion dialog box.

6. The program generates a table according to specifications. 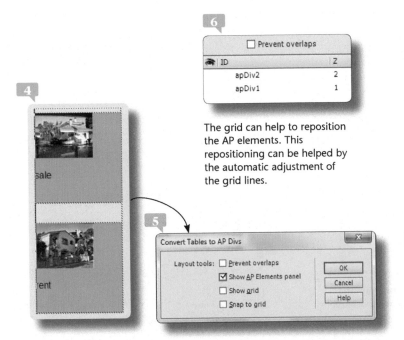 To perform the contrary action, open the **Modify** menu, click **Convert** and select **Tables to AP Divs**.

7. In the **Convert Tables to AP Divs**, disable the **Prevent overlap**, **Show Grid**, and **Snap to Grid** options and click **OK**.

8. An AP element is created for each cell of the table with content. Select the **apDiv1** element in the AP Elements panel, click the **CSS-AP Element** in the **Properties** panel and type **sale**.

9. Enter the value **300px** in the L field box and click **Enter**.

10. Display the **Vis** box and select **Hidden**.

11. In the document window, click the upper-right corner of the **rent** AP element, type the word **rent** in the **CSS-AP Element** field box and click **Enter**.

12. Enter the value **300px** in the L box and select **Hidden** in the **Vis** box to hide the element.

13. Note that the **Hidden** option hides the AP elements only in the browser pre-visualization. Click the page and click **Save** to save the changes.

IMPORTANT

The pixel is the position and size predetermined unit. You can also use picas, points, inches, millimeters, or the corresponding parent element percentage value.

9

10

The program automatically assigns a name to each AP element generated for conversion.

7

8
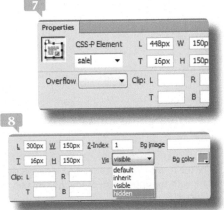

6

☞ ID	Z
apDiv2	2
apDiv1	1

The grid can help to reposition the AP elements. This repositioning can be helped by the automatic adjustment of the grid lines.

Creating forms

IMPORTANT

When the visitor of a web page enters the information required in a web form and clicks the Submit button, the data introduced is automatically sent to the server, which, after processing, returns it to the user or customer.

FORMS MAKE PAGES INTERACTIVE AND TRANSMIT DATA. For forms to function you need to program the task they are intended to accomplish using appropriate language syntaxes. Dreamweaver makes working with forms easier with the options in the Properties panel. To insert a form in a web page you can use the options in the Menu Bar or the buttons in the Form category of the Insert toolbar. A page can have more than one of these elements, represented by visual aids that define the form's outline.

1. Begin by hiding the AP elements in the **contact.html** page. To do this, click the corresponding visibility icons in the **AP Elements** panel. 🔲

2. Insert a form. Open the **Insert** menu, display the **Form** submenu and select the **Form** command. 🔲

3. The outline, which will not show once the page is loaded in the browser, 🔲 appears on the page. In the **Form ID** field box of the **Properties** panel, type the word **application**. 🔲

4. Assigning a name to the form allows references to be made to it as well as control it through a language program. The **application** form lacks content, but you can include common page elements: text, images, tables, etc. Click inside the form

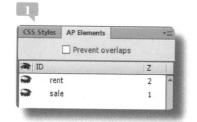

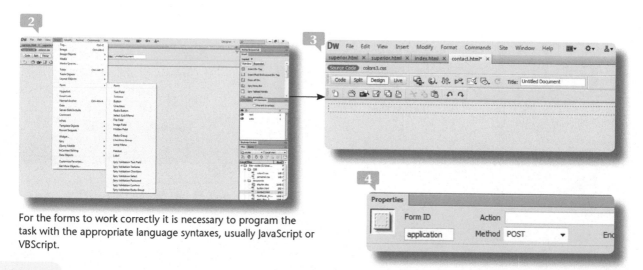

For the forms to work correctly it is necessary to program the task with the appropriate language syntaxes, usually JavaScript or VBScript.

and type the sample phrase **I would like information on homes in:** [5]

5. To design a form you will need to consider the position of the AP elements created in a previous exercise. Display these momentarily to correctly design the form, giving it content. [6]

6. Split the phrase you just entered into two lines, so that the **sale** element doesn't hide part of it. Click the last word, **information**, and click and hold the **Shift** key while pressing **Enter**. [7]

7. Although all kinds of elements can be included in a form, the main components are called **form objects**. Insert a new paragraph at the end of the line, open the **Insert** menu, access the **Form** submenu and select **Checkbox**. [8]

8. Click to the right of the new object, type the word **sale** and click **Enter**. [9]

9. Insert a new check box using a different method. Activate the **Forms** tab in the **Insert** panel and click the **Checkbox** option.

10. Click to the right of the new check box, type the word **rent**, and click **Enter**.

11. In the new paragraph, type the text, **Enter your email here.** Save the changes made and finish the exercise. [10]

IMPORTANT

When you click the first command in the Forms category of the Insert panel, you insert a new form.

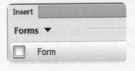

[9]

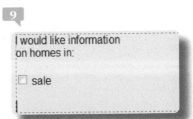

The common mission of all form objects is to receive a user's data.

[10]

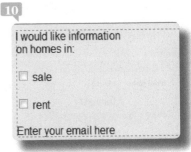

Users can activate or deactivate check boxes.

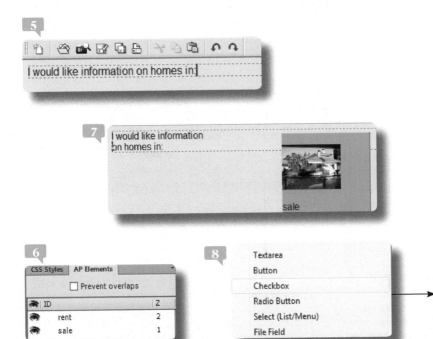

Inserting form objects

EACH FORM OBJECT serves a specific purpose. Text fields accept any alphanumeric value; hidden fields store the information entered by the user that is later retrieved by the user for further usage; and the Multiline option are text field boxes. Check boxes transmit data via identifiers and values. This is also the function of the buttons option, which can be inserted in a group style fashion. In Dreamweaver you can insert a wide range of items in a form, lists and menus, image and game fields, buttons or tags.

1. Click the first check box in the form.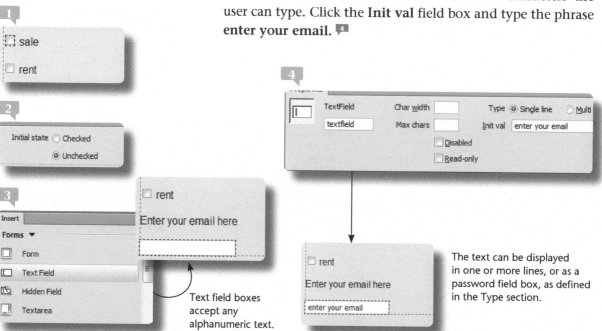

2. In the **Properties** panel you can assign an identifier name to a check box, or click the **Initial State** option in the same panel to change the check box's state. Click the end of the last line of the text and press **Enter** and, in the **Insert** panel, click **Text Field**.

3. The **Text Field** dialog box in the **Properties** panel lets you assign a name to the object. **Char width** determines the maximum number of characters displayed in the field, and **Max chars** determines the maximum number of characters the user can type. Click the **Init val** field box and type the phrase **enter your email**.

IMPORTANT

Jump menus are navigation lists that permit the insertion of a menu where each option is linked to a document or file. **Image Fields** permit the insertion of an image and are generally used to create graphic buttons and **File fields** automatically add a navigation dialog box with its corresponding **Browsing** button to search documents and upload them as form data.

Text field boxes accept any alphanumeric text.

The text can be displayed in one or more lines, or as a password field box, as defined in the Type section.

174

4. Click the document window, located after the text field box, and double-click **Enter.**

5. Press the **Textarea** command of the **Insert** panel and, after verifying which option is editable in the **Properties** panel, click **Delete** to eliminate it from the form.

6. The properties of the **Radio button** object are the same as the check boxes', except for, obviously, the identification field. For the button options in a form to conform as a group, they must have the same identifier assigned to them. In the case of the **Select (List/Menu)**, the **Menu** option displays the values in a menu allowing users the choice of one option only, the **List** option displays the values in a list that users can scroll through to choose several options. The **List Values** opens a dialog box that simplifies the definition of the elements integrating the list or menu. **5** Click the **Button** option in the **Insert** panel. **6**

7. A button with the **Send** tag appears on the screen. **7** Buttons perform actions when they are clicked; in this case a form is submitted. Save the changes and click **F12** to preview the page. **8**

081

IMPORTANT

The **Radio Group** in the Insert panel determines the different option buttons for the group.

Radio Group

In the case of the password field boxes, the typed text is substituted by asterisks or bullets. The **Init Val** field box lets you type the value that will be displayed when the page uploads.

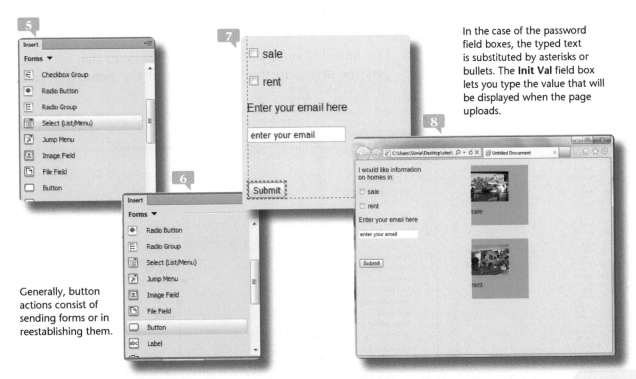

Generally, button actions consist of sending forms or in reestablishing them.

Attaching behaviors

A BEHAVIOR IS A COMBINATION OF AN EVENT and the action triggered by the event. Dreamweaver has over 20 behavior actions, and you can download more from the Exchange for Dreamweaver website. Properties of a selected action are defined in the corresponding dialog box. Events are messages generated by browsers when a user interacts with a site. The program automatically attaches an event to an action in the Behaviors panel.

An action consists of a predetermined JavaScript code that executes a specific task. You can locate more actions from the Adobe website by clicking **Get More Behaviors** in the Exchange for Dreamweaver website.

1. Go to the **AP Elements** panel and hide the two elements of this type that are inserted in the page. 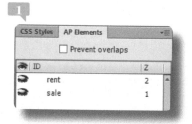 Then, select the first check box in the form, open the **Window** menu and select **Behaviors**.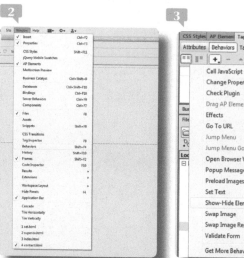

2. The **Tag Inspector** panel lets you insert behavior actions. Press the boxed + and select **Show-Hide Elements**.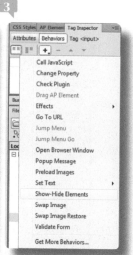

3. This allows you to show or hide AP elements of a document. With the **div "sale"** element selected, click **Show** and click **OK**.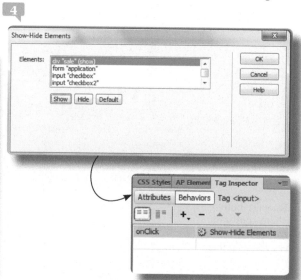

4. Repeat and associate the action needed to display the AP **rent** element for the second check box.

5. Dreamweaver automatically displays the event that best triggers the action in the first column of the **Behaviors** pan-

082

el. Press **onClick** and select **onMouseUp** from the long list of events.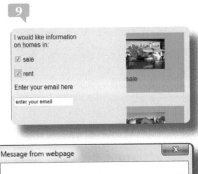

6. In the document window, click the text field contained in the form, select **Add Behavior** and select **Validate Form.**

7. The **Fields** box lists the text fields in the form (in this case, **textfield**). The options in **Accept** specify the correct data type. Select **Email address** and click **OK.**

8. This action is attached to the **onBlur** event that verifies the data as the user completes the form. Or, you can attach it to the **onSubmit** event that verifies when you click the **Submit** button. Save the changes made and preview the page.

9. Click the check boxes to check that the behaviors attached to them function correctly, and do the same for the text validation behavior by typing any word that comes to mind (not a correct e-mail address) in the field and clicking outside the box.

10. The **Validate Form** behavior is executed and an alert pop-up menu appears indicating the value added is incorrect since the field needs to contain an e-mail address. Click **OK** and close the browser to finish.

IMPORTANT

In the **Validate Form** box, the **Anything** option is useful only if **Required** was selected. The **Email address** option verifies that the field contains the @ symbol. The **Number** option verifies that only numbers are included.

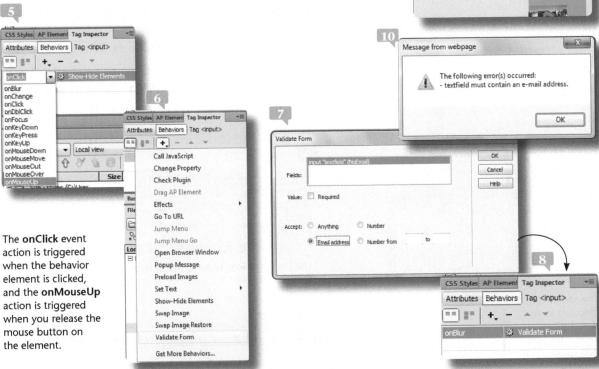

The **onClick** event action is triggered when the behavior element is clicked, and the **onMouseUp** action is triggered when you release the mouse button on the element.

Assigning actions to forms

DREAMWEAVER ASSIGNS THE ACTION OF SENDING A FORM directly to the corresponding button. The data entered in a form can be sent to a web page or an e-mail address. To accomplish this, and after the form is selected, the corresponding action must be defined in the same name field in the Properties panel. This panel also determines the method used to transmit the data to the server as well as the encode type used for processing it. Depending on the selected action in the page codification, possible errors can be corrected directly from the Code view mode of the document.

1. In this exercise you will learn how to transmit the data obtained in a form. Click the **Submit** button. **1**

2. This button shows the **Button** name and the **Value**. **2** The default **Value** action is **Submit**. Click the tag corresponding to the form, **form#application**, on the **Status Bar**. **3**

3. By default the program does not determine any action for the form. To send the data entered to a web page, the path must be specified in the **Action** field or use the folder icon to locate the page. For the form to be sent to an e-mail address, type the expression **mailto:** followed by the address. **4**

4. You also need to define the method used to transmit data to the server. In this case, select the **POST** Method, which will embed the form's data in the HTTP request. There is also the

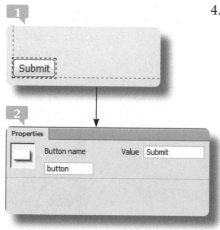

The name functions as an identifier, and the value is the text that appears in it.

Use the folder icon to locate the page where the button should go to when clicked.

Remember that the sample form's name is **application**.

GET option that adds value to the URL requesting the page. Click the **Enctype** field and enter **text/plain**.

5. In doing this, the message body will gather all the data in a simple text line. But for this to function correctly you need to automatically correct the code generated by the program. Click the **Code** button in the **Document** toolbar.

6. The parameters defined in the **Properties** panel are set in inverted comas. Remove the inverted comas from the terms **mailto**, **post,** and **text/plain**.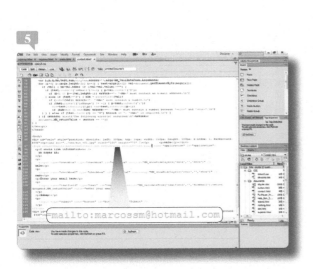

7. Click the **Design** button in the Document toolbar, click **Save** in the Standard toolbar to store the changes made and click **F12** to preview the page.

8. Click the **sale** checkbox and verify the element **sale** is displayed. In addition the activation of the check box also means the assigning of a value that will be transmitted when the form is sent. Enter an e-mail address in the corresponding field and click **Submit**.

9. An alert pop-up indicates the form is being sent by e-mail. Click the **Cancel** button and close the browser and the **contact.html** page.

IMPORTANT

The **Enctype** drop-down menu determines the type of encoding sent to the server for processing. The program offers two types of encoding. The first is usually used together with the POST method. The MIME type is useful only if it has created a file uploading field. In addition to the predetermined codes, you can also use the alternative encodings.

The message generated when the form is submitted collects the e-mail address, entered in the field, in a simple text line.

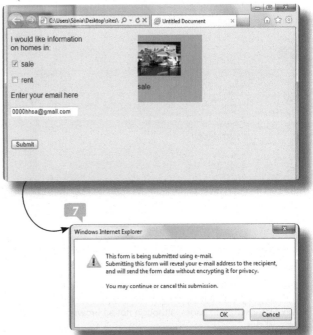

Creating documents in JavaScript

IMPORTANT

To include an external programming script you can also link the external document to the page. Just place the edit cursor where you want to introduce the script and follow the menu path **Insert/HTML/Script Objects/Script** to the **Script** dialog box. Then with the script mark on the page, go to the Properties panel and select the external JavaScript file so the path is included in the **Source** field box.

DREAMWEAVER SUPPORTS different programming languages, such as JavaScript (.js extension documents) and Action Script, the Flash code (.as extension documents). Dreamweaver uses JavaScript language to create behavior. External JavaScript files can be used to add interactivity to pages and can be attached to the page or be embedded in the header to define a function.

1. Copy the JavaScript document, **cerrarventana.js**, available from our web site (it is not necessary to copy it to a site folder). When you have the file ready, click **Ctrl + N** to access the **New Document** dialog box, select **JavaScript** in the **Page Type** section of the **Blank Page** category and click **Create**. 🔲

2. The **Code** view is automatically activated since this type of document cannot be visually edited. 🔲 Click the Close button to exit the document.

3. A Dreamweaver behavior is nothing more than a JavaScript code fragment, a programming language understood by most browsers today. The program offers behaviors to simplify as-

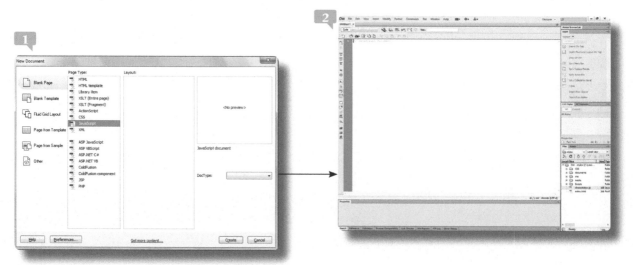

Use the programming language ActionScript, common in Flash programming documents, to assign actions to SWF files inserted in pages, although not all browsers support this.

signing actions, but Dreamweaver also allows the use of external program documents. Open the **sale_01.htm** page from the **Files** panel.

4. In the **Files** panel click the arrow in the **Show** box and locate and double-click the **cerrarventana.js** file.

5. The programming of this JavaScript document targets the performance of one task only, that of closing the browser window. Select and copy lines two through six.

6. Once the mentioned fragment is copied, close the document.

7. Click **Code** in the Document toolbar, place the cursor at the start of the fifth code line and press the **Paste** icon in the Standard toolbar.

8. Once the JavaScript function is defined in the header it can be activated from the page body. In order to do this, a call must be made to the function from an element in the body page that supports this behavior. This will be explained in the next exercise. To finish, click **Design** in the Document toolbar and save the changes.

IMPORTANT

The creation of a text file implies the automatic activation of the Code view, since this type of file cannot be visually edited.

| Code | Split | Design | Live |

JavaScript functions should be included in the header of the page.

The JavaScript document extension is .js.

Calling JavaScript

DREAMWEAVER HAS A PREDETERMINED BEHAVIOR that associates page elements to JavaScript functions that are embedded in the headers. In the Call JavaScript dialog box you need only to define the header function of the page associated with the action. The program assigns an event to the action that can be modified from the Behavior panel. To do this you can either select an event from the program or introduce it directly, using the appropriate syntax, in the field corresponding to the event in that panel.

1. In this exercise you will learn how to call a function by associating a behavior to a body element on the page. Go to our website and copy and save the file image **close.gif** to the **styles** site's **ima** folder. You will insert this image in **sale_01.htm** page. Open the **Insert** menu and select **Image**. 🔲

2. Double-click to open the **ima** folder and locate and select the **close.gif** image and click **OK**. 🔲

3. Next, change the image location. Click and drag it to place it in the lower left part of the table. 🔲

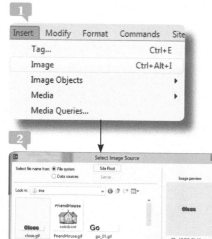

Remember that you can access the Select Image Source dialog box by clicking Ctrl + Alt + I.

4. In the **Behavior** panel click **Add Behaviors** and select **Call JavaScript.**

5. This action leads to the **Call JavaScript** dialog box, where you need only to define the parameter corresponding to the name assigned in the page header to the intended function. For the function to be executed, you need to introduce parenthesis after its name. Type the expression **window.close** in the **Java-Script** field box, with an open and close parenthesis, and click **OK.**

6. The program automatically assigns the **onClick** event to the action. But this event triggers the action when the image is clicked, and what you want is for the action to be triggered after the image is clicked and when the mouse button is released. To modify, click the event in the **Behavior** panel and type **onMouseUp.**

7. With this, every time the user clicks the image, the **close-window** JavaScript function, defining the closing of the browser window, is called. Preview the page to verify the behavior's correct functioning. Click **Ctrl + S** to save the changes and click **F12** to preview the page.

8. **Close** the image.

9. Because it is local navigation, an alert pop-up menu advises you that the page is going to close. Click **Yes** in the alert menu to finish the exercise.

If you know the correct syntax, you can type the event you want to use. All events begin with **on** followed, without spaces, by the **event definition**.

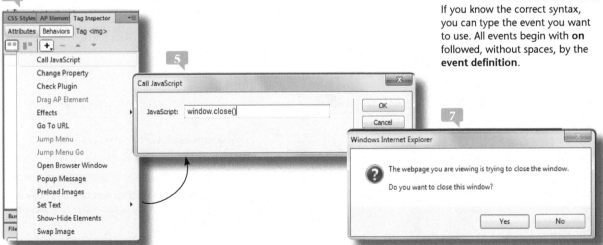

Using hints for JavaScript code

DREAMWEAVER'S CODE hints help you insert the JavaScript code quickly and without mistakes. The CS6 version has improved the support offered to simple data type and central JavaScript objects, while the incorporation of JavaScript frameworks, jQuery, Prototype, and Spry has widened its scope of functionality.

1. The Hint function lets you insert and edit codes quickly and without mistakes. To modify the default settings for code hints, you need to access the Preferences dialog box of the application. Open the **Edit** menu and click **Preferences**.

2. Select **Code Hints** from the category list on the left. ▣

3. **Close Tags** determines how closing tags are inserted. Maintain the Dreamweaver default option that inserts the closing tag automatically after typing the characters </. ▣ Go to **Options** to enable or disable the appearance of code hints or adjust by seconds the timing before they are shown. Move the sliding control of this section until it reaches **1 second**. ▣

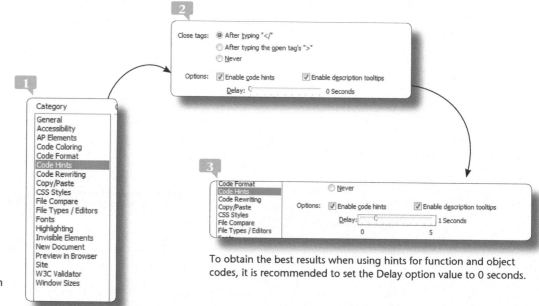

Even if the code hints are disabled, click the key combination Ctrl + Space bar to show in Code view.

To obtain the best results when using hints for function and object codes, it is recommended to set the Delay option value to 0 seconds.

086

4. **Menus** sets the type of code hints you wish displayed while typing. Maintain all the options in this section activated and click **OK** to apply the changes made.

5. If activated, code hints appear automatically when typing in Code view, but you can also display the Hint menu manually, without typing anything. To do this, click the **Split** button in the **Document** Bar to activate the **Split** view.

6. Let's say you want to change the background color of the cell containing the price of the house, by typing the corresponding code for that attribute. Click inside the cell so that the edit cursor is placed in the correct code area.

7. Click after the quotation marks that close value 79 and press the space **bar**.

8. Just as you established in the Preferences dialog box, the element list appears after 1 second (along with names of tags, attributes, actions, etc.). Use the scroll bar or keyboard arrows to scroll up and down the list. In this case select the attribute **bgcolor** and click **Enter** to insert in the code.

9. After inserting the attribute, the code hints display the color chart to choose a background color for the cell. Click a sample and click **Refresh** in the Properties panel to apply the change.

10. Return to **Design** view and click **Save** in the Standard toolbar to complete the exercise.

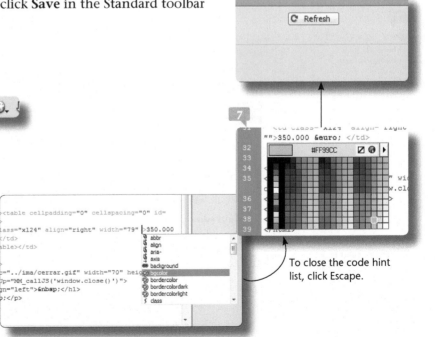

To close the code hint list, click Escape.

Creating editable regions and templates

IMPORTANT

Dreamweaver lets you insert repeating and optional regions. A repeating region is a document section defined to repeat itself; the user uses the repeating region's control options to add or delete copies of the region as it suits the documents based on the template. An optional region is a document section specified optional for content. In the template-based page the user generally controls whether or not the content is shown.

A DREAMWEAVER TEMPLATE is a special type of file that is used to set a page design that can be later used as a base for creating new documents. Pages saved as templates use the .dwt extension. Dreamweaver locks most of the document's regions when it is saved as a template, which means the author should insert editable regions to specify those elements that can be edited.

1. To store the current page as a template, open the **File** menu and select **Save As Template**.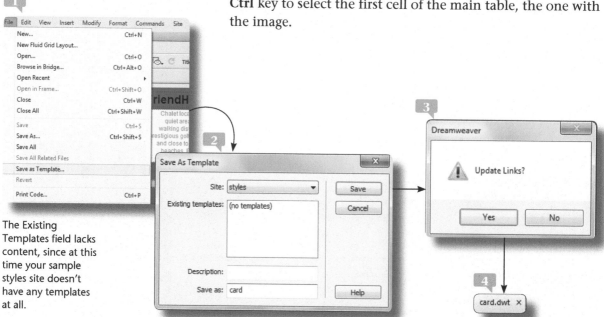

2. Templates should be saved in a site. The program, by default, stores the templates in the site containing the page that served as the base for it. Double-click **Save As**, type the word **card** and **Save**.

3. An alert pop-up menu appears asking to update the links contained in it. Click **Yes**.

4. The template is automatically loaded on the screen, substituting the document that served as the base for it. The document's tab displays the name of the template followed by the .dwt extension corresponding to this type of file. Click the **Ctrl** key to select the first cell of the main table, the one with the image.

The Existing Templates field lacks content, since at this time your sample styles site doesn't have any templates at all.

087

5. When designing a template, the editable regions of the template-based document should be identified. Open the **Insert** menu, display the **Template Objects** submenu and select **Editable Region.**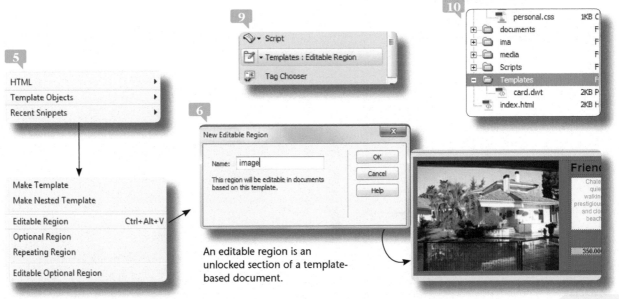

6. In the **Name** field of the **New Editable Region** box type the word **image** and click **OK.**

7. Select the cell containing the building information and enable the **Common** category of the **Insert** panel.

8. Click the arrow point of the **Templates** command in the **Insert** panel and select **Editable Region.**

9. Type the word **info** in the **Name** field box and click **OK.**

10. The editable regions appear in the Design view surrounded by rectangular outlines. In the left upper corner of each region there is a small tab with the corresponding name. Select the nested table in the last cell of the main table, the one containing the price.

11. The **Templates** option of the **Insert** panel now displays the icon corresponding to the editable regions. Click the option, type the word **price** in the **Name** field box and click **OK.**

12. Click **Save** in the **Standard** toolbar and close **card.dwt.**

By default, the program has store the template in the **Templates** folder of your site. Access the **Files** panel to verify this and to locate it in the folder.

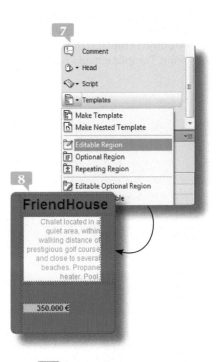

An editable region is an unlocked section of a template-based document.

Creating Template-based documents

IMPORTANT

To unlink a document from a template you need to use the **Modify/Template/Dettach from Template** menu path.

TEMPLATE-BASED DOCUMENTS can be linked to the template itself or function independently, subject to whether the Update Page option is activated or not when the template changes in the New dialog box. The new file's link to the template implies that any changes made to the latter are reflected on the linked page. In this case, the editing of the template-based document is limited to the editable regions of the template, excluding the locked regions. However, if on the contrary, the document is non-template based it can be edited independently.

1. Open the **text.htm** page, access the **New Document** dialog box clicking key combination **Ctrl + N** and activate the **Page from Template** category.

2. Maintain the default option **Update page when template changes** and click **Create**.

3. In this way, any change in the layout of the .dwt document signifies the automatic update of the page. Expand the **text.htm** to the front.

4. Select the information relative to the first rental building located in the nested table in the lower part of the page, copy it  and put the template-based page up front.

In the Site section there is a list of the configured sites. Since your site only has one template, card, this one is automatically selected in the dialog box.

5. Because the page is linked to the originating template, only the editable regions can be modified. The rest of the document can only be altered if the source template is modified or if the page is no longer linked to it. Click the tab of the **info** region and click **Paste**.

6. Select the content of the editable region containing **price**, press the tag and type the value **1500€**.

7. Change the image appearing in the first editable region of the page. Click it and, in the **Source** field box and in the **Properties** panel, substitute, in the file name, the letter **v** for **a** and click **Enter**.

8. In this simple manner you have created a second page describing the building, maintaining the original layout. Press the **Save** icon in the Standard toolbar, type the term **rent_01** as the file name and save in the documents folder.

9. Close the **rent_01.htm** document.

10. Create a link to the **text.htm** page. Click **Ctrl** and, without releasing it, click the cell containing the text **rent offer 000001**.

11. Click the folder icon in the **Link** field box in the **Properties** panel, double-click the **rent_01** page.

12. For the linked page to open in an independent browser window, click the arrow button of the **Target** drop-down menu and select **_blank**.

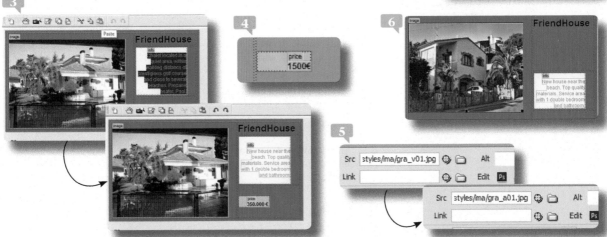

Automating tasks

THE CUSTOMIZED HISTORY PANEL AND COMMANDS allow the automating of tasks. The History panel shows a list of the steps taken in the document until reaching the maximum steps indicated in the program's preferences. This panel lets you undo any of the steps or repeat and create new commands to automate tasks. Steps that can be replayed can be stored as a personalized command. Once a name has been assigned, the program stores it in a configured folder of the system so that it can be executed in any document from the Commands menu.

1. In the **lateral.htm** page of the **styles** site, select the word **contact**.

2. Show the **Behaviors** panel, click **Add Behaviors**, click the **Effects** option and select **Highlight**.

3. In the **Highlight** dialog box enter the value **2000** in the **Effect duration** field box, select a color sample in the **Color After Effect** field and click **OK**.

4. The effect will be replayed when the user clicks on the **contact** link. Click the **Save** icon and click **OK** in the alert dialog box that appears.

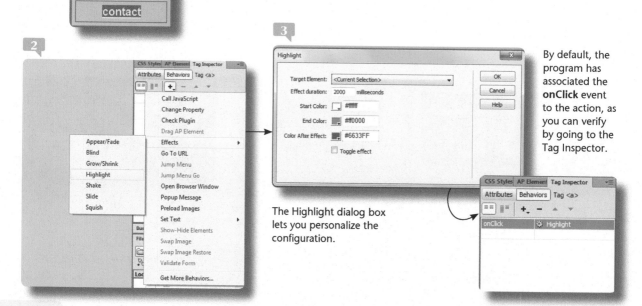

The Highlight dialog box lets you personalize the configuration.

By default, the program has associated the **onClick** event to the action, as you can verify by going to the Tag Inspector.

5. Click **F12** to preview in Internet Explorer and, after clicking the link **contact,** close the document in the browser and verify that the link has acquired the color applied at the end of the effect. ◆ Click the Close button of the browser window to exit.

6. Open the **Window** menu and select the **History** option.

7. In this case the panel recognizes only one step, the step corresponding to the assigning of the behavior to the link. ⑤ Double-click on the word **rent** in the document window.

8. To replay this step it must be selected in the panel. If you click **Replay**, the selected step will replay again. But not all steps can be replayed. For example, the step **Add Behavior** displays a red button with an x symbol indicating it cannot be replayed. Click the **Bold** and **Italic** buttons in the **Properties** panel and double-click the word **sale** in the document window.

9. The replay steps can be applied as a whole. Click the **Apply Bold** step in the **History** panel, click **Shift** and, while holding **Apply Italic,** and press **Replay.** ⑥

10. The panel allows you to store the selected steps as a customized command. Click the **Save** button in the History panel. ⑦

11. In the **Command Name** field box of the **Save As Command** dialog box, type the word **format** and click **OK.** ⑧

12. Double-click the **home** link, open the **Commands** menu and select the **format** option.

13. To finish, close the current page and click **Yes** in the alert pop-up menu.

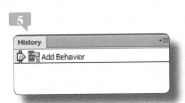

The History panel lets you undo one or more steps, as well as replay the steps and create new commands to automate repeating links.

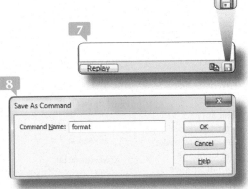

Stored commands are saved permanently in a system folder to maintain the program's configuration, which are saved in the Commands menu.

Creating a Spry Data Set

THE DREAMWEAVER SPRY FRAMEWORK CONSISTS of a JavaScript library that provides web designers with the capability of offering users a more complete web experience. You can use Spry with HTML, CSS, and some JavaScript code to incorporate XML data to HTML documents. You can create widgets (complex interactive elements) and add different types of effects for several page elements. Spry is especially useful for web design professionals or advanced users.

1. Copy the file **planets.xml** from our website and save to your **documents** folder. Close all other documents and create a new HTML document.

2. Before you continue, and to avoid future confusion, save the page to the **styles** site folder. Open the **File** menu and click **Save AS**, locate and open the **styles** folder, assign the name **Spry** to the document and click **Save**.

3. Activate the **Spry** category in the **Insert** panel 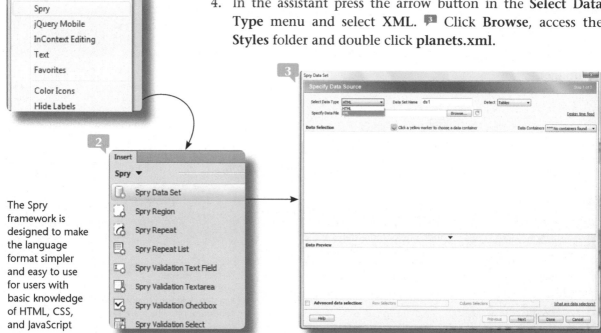 and press the first option, **Spry Data Set**.

4. In the assistant press the arrow button in the **Select Data Type** menu and select **XML**. Click **Browse**, access the **Styles** folder and double click **planets.xml**.

The Spry framework is designed to make the language format simpler and easy to use for users with basic knowledge of HTML, CSS, and JavaScript

090

5. The **Row element** box displays a series of tags related to the selected file, while in the **Data Preview** view you can verify the real preview that will be displayed. Select the **event** tag.

6. Once the data source is specified, you can go to the next screen of the assistant to establish other data options such as column types, order of, and the application or not of a filter for duplicated rows, etc. In this case, click **Done** to create a data set.

7. Verify that the data set selected is displayed in the **Bindings** panel. However, until the data is inserted, the page remains empty. Click **Code** to view the code page.

8. In the code visualization of the document you'll be able to see that the data in reference to the xml file, which you will use to complete the table, has been inserted. You will finish this exercise here, for the moment. Click the **Design** view button to go back to the **Design** view.

9. Click to **Save** the changes made to the new document.

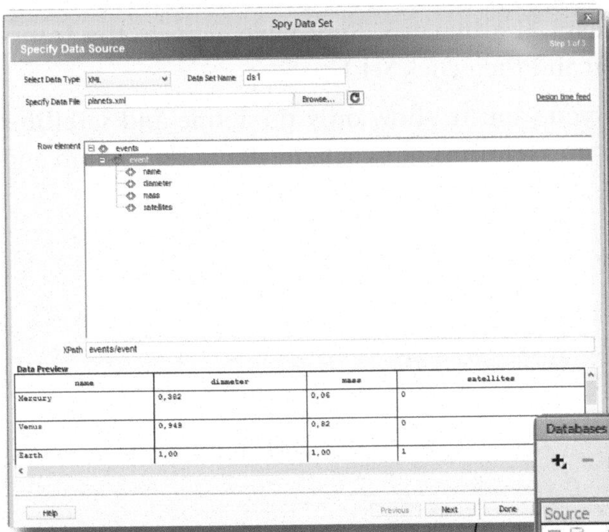

The XML file used as a data set should be stored in the same site as the current document.

193

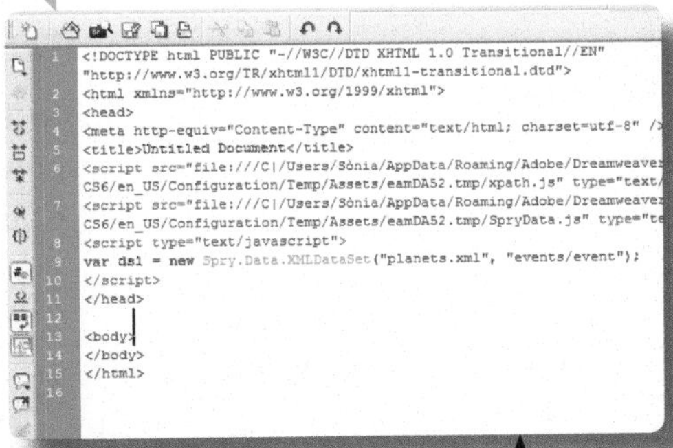

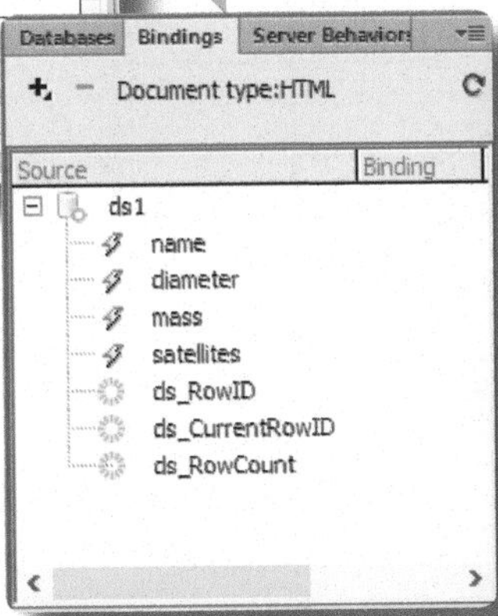

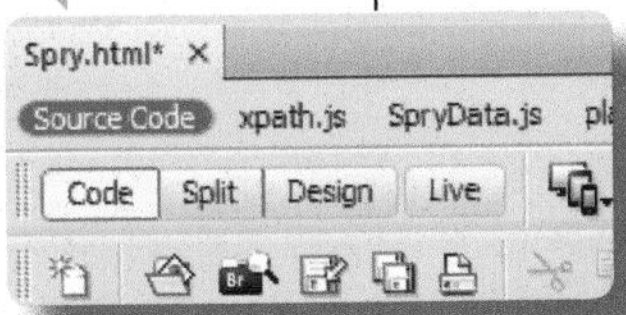

Inserting a Spry table and regions

IMPORTANT

If the HTML page has CSS styles that are associated as an attached style sheet or as an individual style set, you can apply a CSS class for the odd and even rows. You can also apply a Hover Class to change the appearance of a row when you place the cursor over it, and Select Class to modify the appearance of a row when you click it. It is very important for the rules to be in this order (odd, even, hover, select).

THE SELECT INSERTION OPTIONS screen of the assistant to create Spry data determines how the data is displayed. You can use a dynamic table (that allows the dynamic data update of a Dreamweaver page) display or a detailed/master layout, a stacked container layout (in a column) or stacked (two-columns) with a spotlight area.

1. Click the **Spry Data Set** button, the first in the **Insert** panel, and, following the steps detailed in the previous exercise, select the **XML** data type, specify **planets.xml** as the data file and maintain the term **ds2** as the name for the set.

2. In the **Row element** box, select the term **event** and click **Next**.

3. Press **Next** in the Data preview window and go to the layout selection screen.

4. To display data in a dynamic Spry table activate the **Insert Table** option and then click **Set Up.**

5. In this case you want to show only the **name** and **satellites** columns. In the **Columns** box click the **diameter** column and double-click the button with the character –.

6. Verify that the **Sort column when header is clicked** is activated for both columns, activate the **Update detail region when row is clicked**, click OK  and click **Done** to insert the table.

7. In the Dreamweaver work area two columns are displayed without the content. **5** Save the changes made and click **F12** to see the page in the web browser.

8. The table is correctly displayed in the browser and its content is correctly visualized. **6** Click the Close button to exit the browser.

9. Click the **div** tag in the Status Bar to select the entire table **7** and press **Delete**.

10. We will repeat the same process to insert the table, only this time in two columns. In the **Bindings** panel double-click on the **ds2** element. **8**

11. The **Spry Data Set** dialog box re-opens. Select the term **event** and press **Next** twice.

12. In the **Choose Insert Options** screen select **Insert Table** and click **Done**.

13. Notice that the table has been inserted with the four columns that refer to each of the XML document tags. Save the changes and click **F12** to visualize the table in the browser. **9**

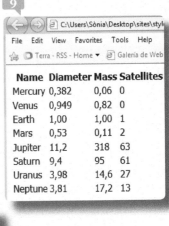

Inserting Spry widgets

IMPORTANT

CSS and JavaScript files associated with a widget receive that widget's name, facilitating the correspondence between files and widgets (for example, the files associated to an accordion widget are called **SpryAccordion.css** and **SpryAccordion.js**).

A SPRY WIDGET CONSISTS OF THREE PARTS: structure, behavior, and style. Structure is an HTML code block that defines the structural composition of the widget. The behavior is the JavaScript language controlling the widget's answer to the events initiated by the user. And style is a CSS style specifying the appearance of the widget itself. Framework behaviors include functions that let the user decide whether to show or hide the content of a page or change its appearance and interact with the elements of a menu, among others.

1. Download the **planets.doc** from our website (you don't have to store it in the current site's folder). In this exercise you will add a panel type widget in tabs with the information split in several tabs. Begin by clicking the **div** tag in the Status Bar and press **Delete**.

2. In the **Insert** panel click **Spry Tabbed Panels**.

3. The **Properties** panel updates displaying the characteristics of this interactive element. In the tabbed panel included in the page, select **tab 1** and type the term **Mercury**.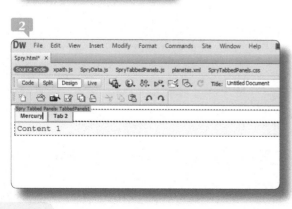

4. Open the **planets.doc** and copy the first information paragraph on Mercury 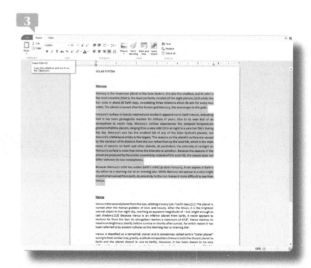 and expand the Dreamweaver document to the front again.

196

5. Return to the tabbed panel, delete the term **Content 1** and, instead, paste the fragment copied.

6. Once the content is pasted in the table, place the cursor on tab 2 and click the icon with the eye image when it appears.

7. When the icon is clicked, the content information displayed on the screen corresponds to tab 2. In this case, you will repeat the above procedure. Change the name of the tab to **Venus** and, in the content area, insert the second paragraph of the text document.

8. Add a third tab to the panel. Click the upper blue tag to see the panel information in the **Properties** panel and click the icon with the + in the Panels menu.

9. A new tab is now added to the panel; double-click it and change the name to **Earth.**

10. Don't add any information to the tab, just erase the text **Content 3.**

11. Visualize the page with the browser. Click **Ctrl+S**, followed by **F12.**

12. In the browser, click the different tabs to see how the content is updated, and close the window.

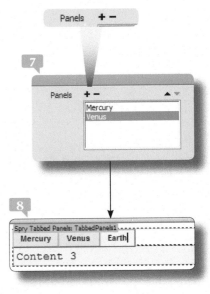

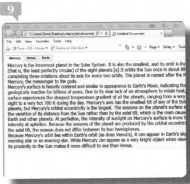

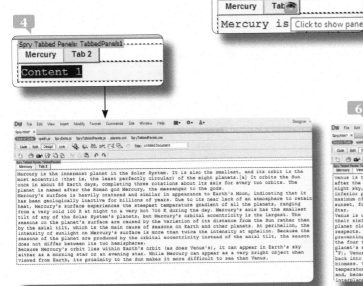

Inserting Spry menu bars

THE SPRY MENU BARS CAN SUBSTITUTE FOR OLD, conventional navigation bars. The function is similar, both allow scrolling up and down the page and files of a site, and provide a global vision of the site's organization.

1. In this exercise you will learn how to insert a menu bar in the **Index** page of the **styles** site. Open the **Files** panel and double-click to select the page.

2. On the **Index** page, press **Enter** in the upper part of the work area, display the **Insert** menu, click the **Spry** command and click **Spry Menu Bar.** 🔲

3. In the **Spry Menu Bar** dialog box select **Horizontal** and click **OK.** 🔲

4. Insert a Menu Bar that, by default, has four items and some sub-items. 🔲 In this case, you want the bar to have three items. In the **Properties** panel click the first icon, **Minus,** 🔲 to delete one item and, in the alert box, click **OK.** 🔲

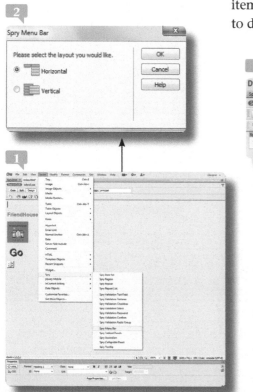

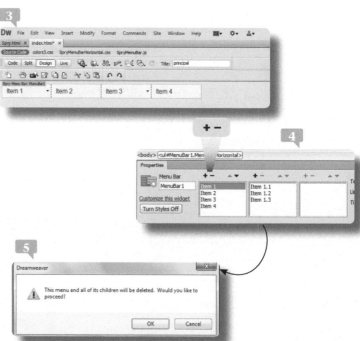

093

5. With item 2 selected, modify the content of the **Text** field introducing the name **Sales**. [6]

6. Below this item are the links to the pages with sales offers. Click the + of the second Item field. [7]

7. In the **Text** field of this item, type the text **Offer01** and see how the item is updated in the Menu Bar. [8]

8. Click the **Link** folder icon and, in the **Select File** dialog box, click the **sale_01.htm** page. [9]

9. Repeat the process with the next item, called **Rent**. Once the name is changed, click, in the submenu field, the – icon twice and, in the **Text** field of the only remaining element, type the text **Offer02**. [10]

10. Click the **Link** folder icon and locate and select **rent_01.htm**.

11. Change the name of the last item, now called **Contact**, and click the **Link** icon folder to select the **contact.htm** page. [11]

12. To finish, click **Ctrl + S** to save the changes made and see the result in the browser.

13. Verify that each element leads to the correct page, [12] and close the browser.

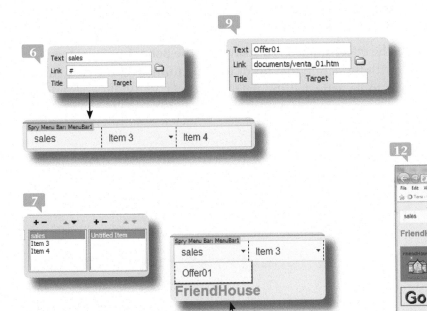

Adding Spry effects

IMPORTANT

Not all effects can be applied to any page element. The Target Element field box alerts to the fact that the action is not possible if the element selected is not a valid target.

SPRY EFFECTS ARE VISUAL IMPROVEMENTS that can be applied on practically any element of an HTML page through JavaScript. They are often used to highlight information, create animated transitions, or visually modify a page during a certain period of time. When applying Spry effects it isn't necessary to use personalized tags. To apply Spry effects the element should be selected or have an ID. The effect modifies opacity, scale, or element position, as well as style properties.

1. As you complete the exercise you will see how simple it is to apply Spry effects in an HTML document. Continue working with the **Index.htm** page on the **styles** site. Select the title of the page, the term **FriendHouse**, to apply a Spry effect.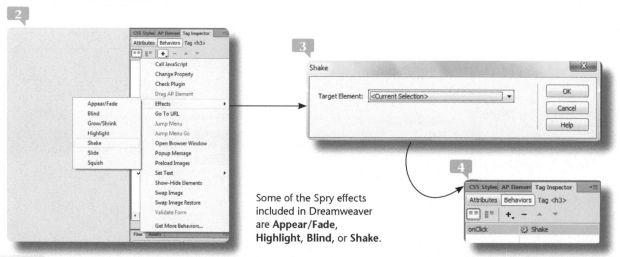

2. In the **Behaviors** panel click the + button, select the **Effects** command and, in the submenu displayed, select the **Shake** effect.

3. This effect shakes the selected element from side to side. Click the **OK** button in the **Shake** dialog box to apply the effect to the current selection.

4. The effect applied is displayed in the **Behavior** panel together with the action that needs to be performed on the element for it to be activated (by default, a click). While maintaining

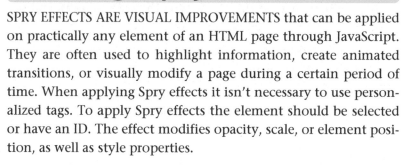

Some of the Spry effects included in Dreamweaver are **Appear/Fade**, **Highlight, Blind,** or **Shake**.

200

094

the **Shake** effect selected in the panel, click the – button and click **Enter** to verify elimination.

5. Click the + button **Effects** and, in the effects submenu select **Appear/Fade**.

6. This effect has several properties settings. By default, the effect fades out the element, but this can be modified to the contrary effect. Display the **Effect** box and click **Appear.**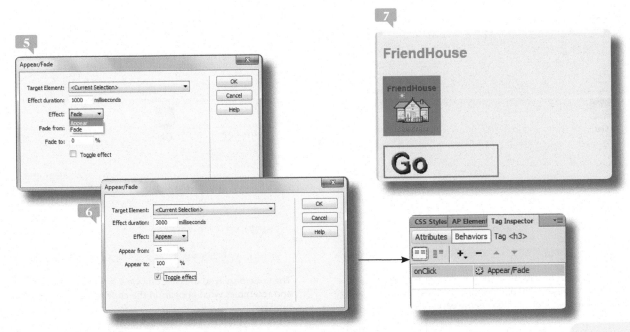

7. In the **Effect duration** field, substitute the value **1000** for the value **3000**.

8. Insert the percentage of transparency from and to the point of the element's appearance. By default, the text appears from nowhere and will be completely visualized, but, in this case, increase the percentage of visibility anyway. Enter the value **15** in the **Appear from** field box.

9. The **Appear to** field box remains at 100%, which means that the text will show completely. Activate the **Toggle Effect** option so that the element appears and fades consecutively, and click **OK** to apply the effect.

10. Click **Ctrl + S** to save the changes made and click **F12** to preview the page in the browser and see the result.

11. Double-click the term **FriendHouse** to verify how the effect appears and, to finish, close the page and browser.

IMPORTANT

You can apply more than one effect to the same element, which can sometimes have interesting visual results.

Working with Live view

IMPORTANT

You can change to Live view when Design view is enabled. The change to Live view is not related to toggling among other view modes (Code, Split, Design). The Live view is therefore a way of choosing between an editable and a "live" mode in the Design view.

THE LIVE VIEW FUNCTION ALLOWS YOU TO DESIGN web pages in the same conditions as a real browser, without ever losing direct code access at any point. Code changes are automatically reflected in the graphic representation shown on the screen.

1. The main difference between the **Live view** and the **Design** view is that it offers a more reliable non-editable representation of the image that the page will have in a browser. This function provides a form of viewing the page in its own Dreamweaver workspace. With the **Index** page of the **styles** site open, click the **Live** button in the **Document Bar**. [1]

2. The functions in the **Properties** panel are now disabled, indicating that Live view doesn't allow the page to be edited. **Live Code** lets you view the code as it will be seen when the code source of the page is displayed in the browser. Click this button. [2]

3. **Live Code** view is dynamic and updates as it interacts with **Live view**. The code is highlighted in yellow and cannot be modified. Try changing one of the values to confirm this. [3]

Live view isn't a substitute for the browser preview, but it allows you to see the appearance of the page when published without exiting Dreamweaver.

The code displayed in Live Code view is non-editable and resembles what appears in the code source from the browser.

4. Click the **Live Code** button to return to the editable code view.

5. The code is now editable. Enter, for example, the value **110** for both the width and height of the image 4 and click **Update** in the **Properties** panel.

6. The arrow point of the **Live view Options** button, located to the right of the Address Bar of the **Document Bar**, hides a series for options of this new visualization mode. To view these options, enable **Live View** and click the button with the same name. 5

7. The **Freeze JavaScript** option lets you freeze elements affected by JavaScript code in their current state while the **Disable JavaScript** option disables JavaScript. The **Disable Plugins** option disables plug-ins and shows the page as is and as it would be displayed in the browser without the activated plug-ins. In addition, Live view lets you use a testing server for the document source, local files for document links and HTTP request settings. Click on the corresponding button to disable **Live View**.

See how the dimensions inserted in the code are now reflected in the Properties panel. 6

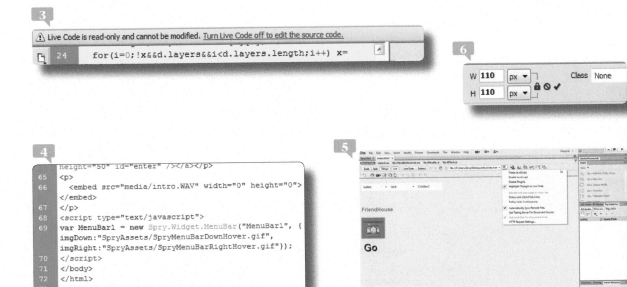

The changes made in the code will automatically be effective in the design after a few seconds.

Inspecting CSS styles

THE INSPECTOR MODE FUNCTIONS TOGETHER with live view to quickly identify HTML elements and associated CSS styles. Enable the inspector mode and run the cursor over the element in question in the CSS dialog box to view its attributes.

1. Open the **styles** site **Index** page and click **Live** view to activate it.

2. When the Live view is enabled the **Inspect** button is automatically added to the **Document Bar**. Click it.

3. The content is framed by a yellow outline indicating the area will be inspected. Move the mouse over the different page elements, but don't click on any of them.

4. See how the information on each element, although not editable, updates in the Properties panel. Click the **Switch now** link in the Alert Bar.

5. This option automatically changes the workspace view, activating the **Split** mode and opening the **CSS Styles** panel. Run

Be aware that the Inspect button appears only when Live view is activated.

the mouse over the elements and watch the information updating in the **CSS Styles** panel.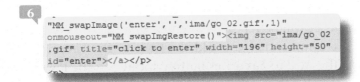

6. The **CSS Styles** panel is divided into three sections. **Summary for Selection** displays the summary of the selected element's properties. Place the mouse on the line separating the first and second section of the panel, click and, while holding, drag down to expand the section's area.

7. With more elements visible in the section, place the mouse on the title **FriendHouse** and watch the data update.

8. The **Rules** section shows the document format information. Pass the mouse across the word **Entrar** and notice the information in that section.

9. As you know, the **CSS inspect** function activates the Live and Code view, which means that every time you run the mouse over an element the code is highlighted.  To complete the exercise click to disable **Live** view and **Code** view and then return to **Design** view.

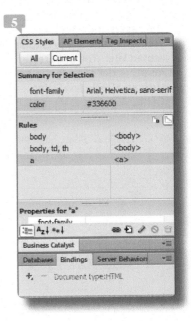

```
"MM_swapImage('enter','','ima/go_02.gif',1)"
onmouseout="MM_swapImgRestore()"><img src="ima/go_02
.gif" title="click to enter" width="196" height="50"
id="enter"></a></p>
```

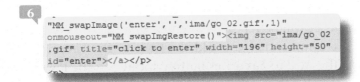

When you enable the CSS Inspect function, it automatically activates Live and Code view.

Working with the Assets panel

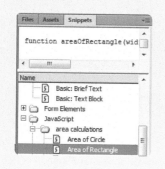
USE THE ASSETS PANEL TO keep track of and obtain previews of the assets stored in a site (images, movies, colors, scripts, and links). The Assets panel also lets you insert assets in pages that are being edited. By default, the panel displays the active Site view, listing a site's total assets. You can store a file in a different site than the one being edited, adding the file to the Favorites list of the target site. You can also locate the assets in the system's folder of the site being edited.

1. Start the exercise with a new blank page. Click the icon in the **Assets** panel to display it on the screen. **1**

2. The panel classifies the assets in categories according to format. The first category lists the site's stored image files alphabetically by name. Click the **FriendHouse.gif** asset icon and press **Insert**. **2**

3. The image file is inserted in the page. **3** If the insertion of an asset will be repeated when editing the site's documents, it is recommended you add the asset to the **Favorites** list. Click the **Add to Favorites** button, located in the lower part of the Assets panel and click **OK** when the pop-up menu appears. **4**

4. In the Assets panel, click **Favorites**. **5**

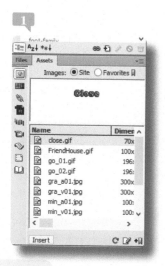

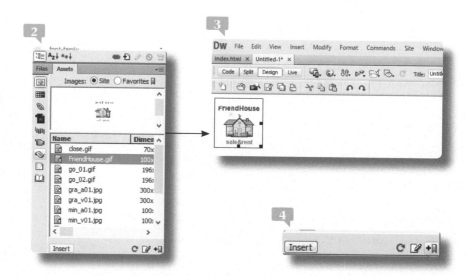

5. Click the Options menu icon in the **Assets** panel, click **Copy to Site** and select the **Elemental** site.

6. The file is now integrated in the Favorites list of the indicated site. Click **OK** in the alert box.

7. The buttons on one side of the **Assets** panel show various categories of files. Re-activate the **Site** option and click the second button, **Colors**.

8. This category lists the colors already applied to the site's pages and those included in its style sheets. Click the **URL** button, the third button in the group.

9. You can assign a link to the selected element of the page. The panel includes only external links to a site's pages. Select the last link of the Assets list that begins with the expression **mailto** and click **Apply**.

10. The image is now linked to the e-mail address indicated. External links can be stored in sites. In the **Assets** panel, right-click the link's icon, click **Copy to Site** and select the **Elemental** site.

11. Click the **SWF** button, the fourth in the button group, and verify that the Assets list includes only the SWF documents stored on the site and not the FLA source files.

12. The other categories, and in this order, include, Shockwave files, videos, external scripts, created templates, and library elements. To complete the exercise, click the **Save** icon in the Standard toolbar and store this page in the root folder of the **styles** site.

IMPORTANT

The removal or adding of an asset will not appear in the Assets panel until you click the Update button and update the Site list.

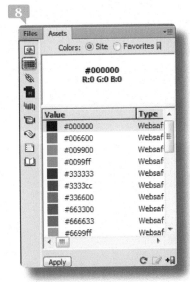

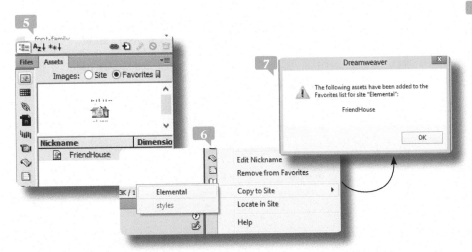

Editing library elements

IMPORTANT

If a library item was created by the insertion of assets in a page, to function correctly in another site after being copied, you must also copy the assets to the library item's target site.

TEMPLATES AND LIBRARY ITEMS are assets that are linked. When you edit an item you also update the documents using them. Library elements are conceived as individual design items, while templates allow you to control the design of an entire page.

1. Select and hold the image, open the **Modify** menu, click **Library** and select **Add Object to Library.**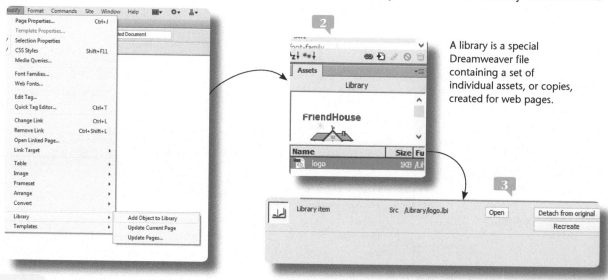

2. The creation of a library item means its inclusion in the site's Assets list. The **Assets** panel lets you assign a name to the item. Type the term **logo** in the text field box and press **Enter.**

3. The selected item is considered an instance of the **logo** library asset. To detach it, click **Detach from original** in the **Properties** panel.

4. The object retains its original format and can now be edited independently. Click **OK** in the alert pop-up menu.

5. The library item created remains on the site's Assets list and can be used in other pages and stored in other sites. Right-click the library object, **logo**, click **Copy to Site** and select **Elemental**.

6. Close the current page and press the **No** button in the alert pop-up menu.

7. Dreamweaver stores library items in the **Library** folder inside

A library is a special Dreamweaver file containing a set of individual assets, or copies, created for web pages.

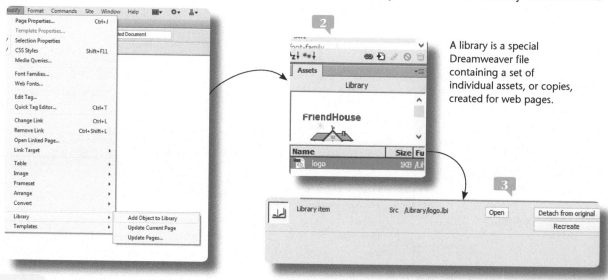

098

the root folder of the local site. The **styles** site acquired the folder with the creation of the library item. In the **Files** panel select the **Elemental** site.

8. Each site has its own library. The **Elemental** site acquired its own Library folder when the **logo** asset was copied. Press the boxed **+** preceding the folder's icon and double-click the **logo.lbi** document.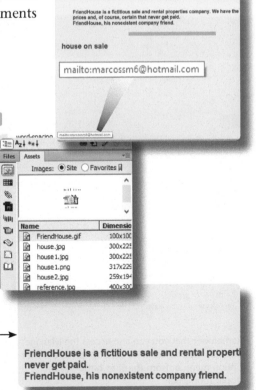

9. The item opens in a new page. Open the **index.htm** page in the **Elemental** site and delete the term **FriendHouse** from the first line.

10. Expand the **Assets** panel and, with the **logo** item selected, click the **Insert** button in the same panel.

11. Access the **URL** and **Image** categories in the **Assets** panel to see the items stored in it.

12. Press the key combination **Ctrl + S** to save the changes made and click **F12** to preview the page.

13. The image is correctly visualized. Click the image to verify that the e-mail link works correctly.

14. A new e-mail message is created with the address already filled in. Close the message and browser window and all documents to finish the exercise.

IMPORTANT

If you wish to use an item repeatedly in the pages of a site, it is recommended that you convert it in a library item and insert instances of the same in pages. This way, the editing of the library item will mean the automatic modification of all the instances used in the site's pages.

The file extension .lbi identifies library items.

209

Setting up a remote site

IMPORTANT

A new feature in Dreamweaver CS6 is the integration of the PhoneGap Build Service in the program. With PhoneGap you can create and simulate applications for mobile devices for various application environments such as Android, IOS, or BlackBerry. To access this service go to the Site menu.

PhoneGap Build Service	Ctrl+Alt+B
PhoneGap Build Settings	Ctrl+Alt+Shift+B

DREAMWEAVER LETS YOU TRANSFER FILES TO REMOTE servers to publish your site's files on the Internet. The Remote Data category of the site's Definition dialog box determines what technology will be used to transfer files. You should also establish the options related to the use of the dynamic testing servers, the protection and hiding of documents, the disposition of the columns in the Files panel, and the site's compatibility with the Contribute technology.

1. Start by accessing the Settings dialog box of the **styles** site. Open the **Site** menu and select **Manage Sites**.

2. Select the **Styles** site and click **Edit**. 1

3. In earlier exercises you defined the settings of the local site: name and local root folder. Activate the **Servers** category and click **Add New Server**. 2

4. To create a remote site all you need to do is to select how you will access the remote server, which is dependent on the technology used for the transmission of local files to the remote server. In this case, maintain the default option **FTP** in

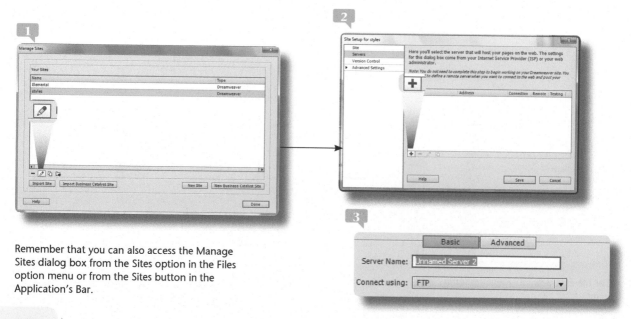

Remember that you can also access the Manage Sites dialog box from the Sites option in the Files option menu or from the Sites button in the Application's Bar.

099

the **Connect using** menu. The access selection depends on the technology supported by the remote server and the one used for creating the site's documents. Your Internet service provider, the one that provides space on the remote server to publish your site, should facilitate the data needed for a correct connection. In the case of FTP connections, you need to have the server's address. In the **FTP Address, User,** and **Password** text box fields, enter the information the service provider gave you.

5. Dreamweaver stores the password so that you don't have to type it each time you wish to access the remote server via FTP. The validity of the data can be tested by clicking the **Test** button.

6. Once the testing is done you can determine in which folder of the remote server you will store the files. Click the **More Options** section to see the setting options.

7. Since the settings of these options will depend on the server type used by each user, click **Save.**

8. The new server will appear defined in the **Site Setup for styles** dialog box. To complete the exercise click **Done.**

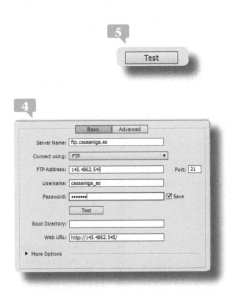

The data required to connect with the remote server should be provided by your Internet service provider. The user name is confidential data that will give you access to the server space reserved for your site.

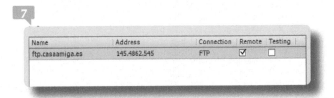

Putting and getting files

THE ACT OF TRANSFERRING A FILE FROM A LOCAL SITE to a remote site is called get, and put is the opposite. To transfer files you first need to connect to a remote server using the Connect to Remote Server button in the Files panel. Once connected the remote site files are listed on the left side of the panel and the local site files to the right. Dreamweaver allows you to edit remote site files, although it is best to edit them locally.

1. The **Files** panel lets you connect and transfer files to the remote site. Display the panel and press the first button, **Connect to Remote Server.**

2. You should have an Internet connection for this to work correctly. To expand the **Files** panel and display the remote and local sites, click the last icon of the panel.

3. When connecting with the server, the program lists the folders of the remote site on the left side of the panel. Select the **index.htm** page of the local site, on the right side of the panel, open the **Site** menu and select **Put.**

4. Before you check in the file, the program displays a dialog box asking permission to include the dependent files of the document that is going to be transferred, as well as the image files inserted. Click **No.**

Once you click the **Connect to Remote Server** button, it automatically changes the icon and becomes instead the **Disconnect from Remote Server** button.

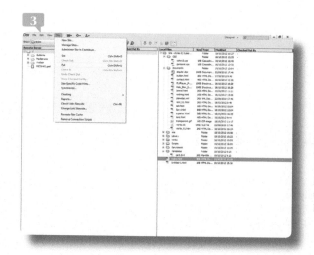

It is recommended that you to check in the entire site to preserve its internal structure, but you can also upload the files individually.

5. A copy of the **index.htm** page is kept on the remote server. Dreamweaver lets you edit directly by double-clicking the files that are not blocked from the remote site. To transfer the entire local site to the server, select the root folder from the local site and press the **Put file(s) to Remote server** button with an arrow pointing upward.

6. Click **OK** in the confirmation dialog box.

7. The site's files transfer to the server. To facilitate the downloading of files when users visit the website, it is better for the files to be small. Once the process is completed, click the boxed + preceding the **documents** folder of the remote site. Repeat this with the **media** folder to verify the files were transferred properly.

8. Remember that all the files, not just the pages, used in a site must be put on the remote site for it to be correctly visualized. Click the **Disconnect** button, located to the right of the **Show** dialog box and click **Expand/Collapse** to collapse the panel.

9. From now on, when a user accesses the Internet address provided by the service provider of your remote site, the main page of your site will be loaded in the browser. To finish the exercise, click the arrow button in the **View** drop-down menu and select **Local** view.

IMPORTANT

Check in is the transfer of local files to a remote server. Check out is the transfer of remote server files to the local site. You can carry out both actions from the Files menu or the toolbar.

The files of a remote site can be transferred to a local site. Just select the file in the remote site and click the **Get** command in the **Files** menu, or the **Get Files** button represented by the image of an arrow pointing up.

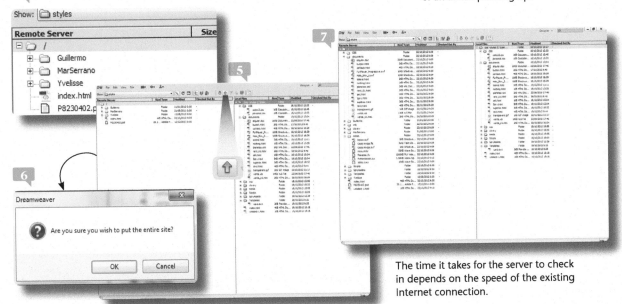

The time it takes for the server to check in depends on the speed of the existing Internet connection.

To continue learning...

This book is part of a collection that covers the most commonly used and known software in all professional areas.

All the books in the collection share the same aproach as the one you have just finished. So, if you would like to know more about other software packages, on the next page, you will find other books in this collection.

OPERATING SYSTEMS

If you are interested in operating systems, then *Learning Windows 8 Consumer Preview with 100 practical exercises* is, without a doubt, the book that you are looking for.

Microsoft is launching a new version of its Windows operating system, which is full of new additions that are both visual and functional. You'll will see the biggest change as soon as you open the program: you are presented with a new personalized screen, giving you direct access to the Metro programs and applications, which you can set up on the PC and where it's possible to access the traditional desktop. The new Metro interface has been designed for touch screen devices.

With this book:

- Practice with the Windows Explorer Ribbon.
- Work with the renewed and advanced Task Manager.
- Use the new security and maintenance tools so that your PC will always be as protected as much as possible.

ILLUSTRATION

If you are more interested in illustrations, your ideal book would be *Learning Illustrator CS6 with 100 practical exercises*.

Illustrator is Adobe's vector-based drawing application that is an excellent tool for computer-aided design. Thanks to its incredible and powerful features, you can create original artwork by using it for pictures and drawings.

Within this book, you will learn to::

- Draw realistic brushstrokes with the new configurable bristle brushes
- Trace the most varied shapes
- Convert simple 2D drawings to incredible 3D objects
- Combine and edit shapes in order to obtain complex ones
- Draw realistic scenes in perspective

COLLECTION LEARNING. . . WITH 100 PRACTICAL EXERCISES

IN PREPARATION. . .

DESIGN AND ASSISTED CREATIVITY

- InDesign CS6
- Flash CS6
- Illustrator CS6
- Image Retouch with Photoshop CS6
- Learning to make your first web 2.0

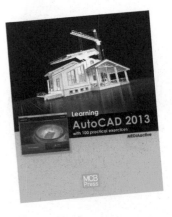